The ULTIMATE Teacher's Book of Lists

MW00635376

More than **250** timesaving lists for today's busy teacher!

Lists for...

long-vowel digraphs

word families

high-frequency words

read-alouds

math facts

math formulas

influential Americans

inventors

animal groups

weather

words of praise

and incentives

...and tons more topics!

Save time planning and preparing teaching materials!

Managing Editor: Jennifer Bragg

Editorial Team: Becky S. Andrews, Diane Badden, Kimberley Bruck, Karen A. Brudnak, Pam Crane, Chris Curry, Amy Erickson, Pierce Foster, Tazmen Hansen, Marsha Heim, Lori Z. Henry, Debra Liverman, Kitty Lowrance, Tina Petersen, Gerri Primak, Mark Rainey, Greg D. Rieves, Kelly Robertson, Hope Rodgers-Medina, Rebecca Saunders, Hope Taylor Spencer, Donna K. Teal, Sharon M. Tresino, Zane Williard

www.themailbox.com

©2012 The Mailbox® Books
All rights reserved.
ISBN 978-1-61276-154-1

Table of Contents

Social Studies

Science

Miscellaneous

 FREE Online Extras!

Follow these steps to get your **FREE** online extras!
  1. Go to www.themailbox.com.
  2. Click on "Register."
  3. Register your copy of *The Ultimate Teacher's
     Book of Lists*. Your item number is 61339.

Phonics Terms

affix: a prefix or a suffix attached to a base word

alliteration: the repetition of a beginning sound in a phrase or sentence
Example: /b/; The big bear buried a bushel of berries.

consonant blend: a combination of two or more letters that are blended together where each sound can still be heard (also known as a consonant cluster)

decoding: translating letters into spoken sounds; another way of sounding out words
Example: A student sees the word *man* and reads /m/-/a/-/n/.

digraph: two letters that stand for one speech sound
Example: /ch/ in *chin*

diphthong: a single vowel sound that glides into another vowel sound within the same syllable
Examples: *oi* in *noise*, *oy* in *toy*, *ou* in *mouse*, and *ow* in *cow*

grapheme: the letter or letters that stand for a phoneme
Example: *B* is the grapheme for /b/.

homograph: two or more words that are spelled the same but sound different and have different meanings
Example: *bow* (as in a hair accessory) and *bow* (as in the front of a ship)

morpheme: the smallest unit in a word that can carry a meaning
Examples: *Walked* has two morphemes, *walk* and *-ed*, to indicate past tense; *dogs* has two morphemes, *dog* and *-s*, to indicate more than one.

onomatopoeia: using a word whose sound imitates its meaning
Examples: *squeak* or *thud*

onset: the initial consonant sound of the syllable
Examples: *t* in *tag* and *sw* in *swan*

phoneme: the smallest unit of sound that is heard in words; a *phoneme* distinguishes one word from another
Examples: /b/ in *bat* and /m/ in *mat* or /a/ in *pat* and /o/ in *pot*

phonemic awareness: the ability to hear, identify, and manipulate phonemes in spoken words

phonics: the relationship between written letters and spoken sounds; the study of letter-sound correspondences

phonological awareness: the recognition of various speech sounds such as syllables, rhymes, onsets, and rimes

prefix: an affix attached at the beginning of a base word

r-controlled vowel: a change in the vowel sound when the letter *r* immediately follows the vowel
Examples: *cat* compared to *car*, *fox* compared to *for*, and *kite* compared to *tire*

rime: the vowel and any remaining consonants in a word or syllable
Example: *op* in *stop*

suffix: an affix attached at the end of a base word

syllable: a word part that contains a vowel or, in spoken language, a vowel sound

word family: a group of words that have different onsets but the same rime

Short Vowels

a	**e**	**i**	**o**	**u**
ax	bed	big	block	bug
back	dress	drip	chop	dust
fan	egg	gift	cot	fun
fast	end	hit	doll	gum
flag	fell	lip	drop	hug
hand	hen	miss	fox	jug
mad	leg	pig	frog	mud
plan	neck	rip	lock	pump
ramp	press	six	mop	run
trap	smell	skip	rock	stuck
van	then	stick	sock	sun
wag	yes	this	stop	up

 # Long Vowels With Silent *e*

a	**e**	**i**	**o**	**u**
came	Pete	bite	bone	cube
face		five	home	cute
gave		life	hope	fume
make		like	joke	fuse
name		mine	nose	huge
plane		nice	note	mule
same		ripe	robe	mute
space		smile	rode	use
tale		time	smoke	yule
wave		wide	vote	

Long-Vowel Digraphs

ai	**ay**	**ea**	**ee**
bait	clay	beach	bee
braid	day	beat	deep
chain	gray	clean	free
fail	hay	eat	green
faint	lay	heal	jeep
laid	may	leap	knee
main	play	meal	meet
nail	ray	peach	need
pail	say	ream	queen
rain	spray	seal	seed
snail	stay	teach	sheep
wait	way	wheat	tree

ie /ē/	**igh**	**oa**	**ow**
believe	bright	boat	blow
brief	fight	coach	crow
chief	fright	coast	flown
piece	high	float	grow
thief	knight	goal	known
	light	groan	low
ie /ī/	might	load	mow
die	night	moan	row
lie	right	road	slow
pie	sigh	soap	snow
tie	sight	toad	throw
vie	tight	toast	tow

R-controlled Vowels

ar
arm
bar
barn
car
card
far
farm
hard
harm
jar
tar
yarn

er
clerk
fern
germ
her
herd
kernel
merge
nerve
serve
swerve
term
verse

ir
bird
birth
circle
dirt
fir
girl
shirt
sir
stir
swirl
third
twirl

or
born
fork
form
fort
horse
morning
porch
sport
stork
storm
torn
worn

ur
blur
burn
curl
fur
hurt
nurse
purr
purse
spurt
turkey
turn
turtle

Word Families

-ack	-ag	-ail	-ain
back	bag	bail	gain
lack	gag	fail	lain
pack	lag	jail	main
quack	nag	mail	pain
rack	rag	nail	rain
sack	sag	pail	vain
tack	tag	rail	brain
black	wag	sail	chain
clack	brag	tail	drain
crack	drag	flail	plain
snack	flag	snail	stain
track	snag	trail	train

-ake	-an	-and	-ank	-ap
bake	ban	band	bank	cap
cake	can	hand	rank	lap
fake	fan	land	sank	map
lake	man	sand	tank	nap
make	pan	bland	yank	tap
rake	ran	brand	blank	yap
take	tan	gland	clank	clap
wake	van	grand	crank	flap
brake	bran	stand	drank	snap
flake	plan	strand	frank	trap
shake	span		plank	scrap
snake	than		thank	strap

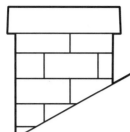

Word Families

-at	-ate	-aw	-ay
bat	date	caw	day
cat	fate	gnaw	hay
fat	gate	jaw	lay
hat	hate	law	may
mat	late	paw	pay
pat	mate	raw	ray
rat	rate	saw	say
sat	crate	claw	clay
brat	grate	draw	play
chat	plate	flaw	stay
flat	skate	slaw	tray
that	state	straw	spray

-eat	-ed	-eep	-ell	-est
beat	bed	beep	bell	best
feat	fed	deep	cell	nest
heat	led	jeep	fell	pest
meat	red	keep	sell	rest
neat	wed	peep	tell	test
seat	bled	seep	well	vest
bleat	bred	weep	yell	west
cheat	fled	creep	dwell	zest
cleat	shed	sheep	shell	chest
pleat	sled	sleep	smell	guest
treat	sped	steep	spell	quest
wheat	shred	sweep	swell	

Word Families

-ice	-ick	-ight	-ill
dice	kick	fight	bill
lice	lick	light	fill
mice	nick	might	gill
nice	pick	night	hill
rice	sick	right	pill
vice	brick	sight	will
price	chick	tight	chill
slice	click	bright	drill
spice	quick	flight	grill
twice	stick	fright	skill
splice	thick	knight	spill
thrice	trick	slight	thrill

-in	-ine	-ing	-ink	-ip
bin	dine	ding	link	dip
fin	fine	king	mink	hip
pin	line	ring	pink	lip
sin	mine	sing	rink	rip
win	nine	wing	sink	sip
chin	pine	bring	wink	tip
grin	tine	cling	blink	clip
shin	vine	sting	clink	drip
skin	shine	swing	drink	flip
spin	spine	thing	stink	ship
thin	whine	spring	think	skip
twin	shrine	string	shrink	trip

Word Families

-it	-ock	-og	-op
bit	dock	bog	cop
fit	lock	cog	hop
hit	mock	dog	mop
kit	rock	fog	pop
lit	sock	hog	top
pit	block	jog	chop
sit	clock	log	crop
flit	flock	clog	drop
grit	frock	flog	flop
knit	knock	frog	plop
skit	shock	smog	shop
spit	stock		stop

-ot	-uck	-ug	-ump	-unk
cot	buck	bug	bump	bunk
dot	duck	dug	dump	dunk
got	luck	hug	hump	funk
hot	muck	jug	jump	gunk
lot	puck	lug	lump	hunk
not	tuck	mug	pump	junk
pot	cluck	rug	clump	punk
rot	pluck	tug	grump	sunk
knot	shuck	chug	plump	chunk
plot	stuck	plug	slump	stunk
shot	truck	slug	stump	trunk
spot	struck	shrug	thump	shrunk

Phonological Awareness and Phonics

Diphthongs

au	oi	ou
auto	boil	about
autumn	broil	cloud
because	choice	found
caught	coin	house
daughter	foil	mouth
fault	join	noun
sauce	point	our
taught	spoil	round
taut	toil	shout
vault	voice	south

aw	oy	ow
claw	annoy	brow
crawl	boy	brown
dawn	cowboy	crowd
draw	decoy	down
hawk	employ	flower
jaw	joy	gown
lawn	loyal	how
paw	royal	now
saw	soy	power
straw	toy	town

oo Words

/ŏŏ/ as in *book*	/ōō/ as in *school*
cook	choose
foot	cool
good	food
hood	moo
look	moon
nook	pool
rook	room
stood	root
took	soon
wood	tool

Initial Consonant Blends

bl	**cl**	**fl**	**gl**	**pl**
black	clap	flag	glad	place
blade	clear	flew	glass	plan
bleed	clip	flip	glide	please
blind	clock	float	globe	plot
block	close	flop	glow	plug
blue	club	fly	glue	plum

sl	**br**	**cr**	**dr**	**fr**
slam	brain	crack	drag	free
sled	bright	crib	dream	friend
sleep	bring	crop	dress	frog
slip	broke	crunch	drill	from
slope	broom	crust	drop	front
slug	brush	cry	dry	fry

gr	**pr**	**tr**	**sc**	**sk**
grab	press	train	scale	skate
grape	price	trap	scan	skill
green	prince	tree	scare	skin
grin	prod	trick	scoop	skip
groan	proud	true	scope	skirt
grub	pry	trust	scout	skunk

sm	**sn**	**sp**	**st**	**sw**
smart	snail	space	stage	swallow
smash	snap	speed	stamp	swap
smell	sneak	spend	step	sweet
smile	snip	spin	stick	swell
smoke	snob	spoil	stir	swim
smooth	snow	spot	stop	swing

scr	**spl**	**spr**	**str**	
scrap	splash	spray	strap	
scream	splendid	spread	stretch	
screw	splint	spring	strike	
script	splinter	sprinkle	string	
scroll	split	sprint	strong	
scrub	splurge	sprout	struck	

Final Consonant Blends

ct	ld	lf	lk	lp
act	build	elf	bulk	alp
conflict	child	golf	elk	gulp
duct	field	gulf	hulk	help
exact	held	self	milk	pulp
insect	mild	shelf	silk	scalp
perfect	world	wolf	sulk	yelp

lt	mp	nd	ng	nk
belt	bump	band	bang	bank
colt	camp	blend	bring	honk
felt	chimp	end	hung	junk
guilt	pump	mind	long	pink
salt	stamp	pond	thing	sunk
tilt	wimp	pound	wing	thank

nt	pt	sk	sp	st
bent	accept	ask	clasp	best
chant	adapt	brisk	crisp	cast
front	adopt	desk	gasp	dust
hint	kept	disk	grasp	first
point	slept	mask	rasp	list
want	tempt	tusk	wisp	lost

Initial Digraphs

ch	**ph**	**sh**	**th**	**wh**
chain	phantom	shade	thank	whale
champ	pharmacy	shark	that	what
chat	phase	shed	the	wheat
cheese	phew	shin	then	wheel
chew	phoenix	shirt	thin	when
chin	phone	shoe	thing	which
chip	phony	shop	think	while
chop	phooey	short	those	whip
chow	photo	show	thud	whisker
chunk	physical	shun	thump	white

Ending Digraphs

ch	**ck**	**sh**	**th**
bench	back	bush	bath
coach	block	cash	birth
crunch	brick	crash	both
each	clock	dish	earth
inch	deck	flesh	fifth
march	lock	gosh	month
much	rock	leash	north
porch	sick	marsh	path
speech	stack	push	tooth
teach	tuck	wash	truth

High-Frequency Words: Grade 1
Fry Instant Words

the	were	time
of	we	has
and	when	look
a	your	two
to	can	more
in	said	write
is	there	go
you	use	see
that	an	number
it	each	no
he	which	way
was	she	could
for	do	people
on	how	my
are	their	than
as	if	first
with	will	water
his	up	been
they	other	called
I	about	who
at	out	am
be	many	its
this	then	now
have	them	find
from	these	long
or	so	down
one	some	day
had	her	did
by	would	get
words	make	come
but	like	made
not	him	may
what	into	part
all		

High-Frequency Words: Grade 2
Fry Instant Words

over	too	men
new	means	read
sound	old	need
take	any	land
only	same	different
little	tell	home
work	boy	us
know	following	move
place	came	try
years	want	kind
live	show	hand
me	also	picture
back	around	again
give	farm	change
most	three	off
very	small	play
after	set	spell
thing	put	air
our	end	away
just	does	animals
name	another	house
good	well	point
sentence	large	page
man	must	letters
think	big	mother
say	even	answer
great	such	found
where	because	study
help	turn	still
through	here	learn
much	why	should
before	asked	America
line	went	world
right		

High-Frequency Words: Grade 3
Fry Instant Words

high	seemed	state
every	next	once
near	hard	book
add	open	hear
food	example	stop
between	beginning	without
own	life	second
below	always	later
country	those	miss
plants	both	idea
last	paper	enough
school	together	eat
father	got	face
keep	group	watch
trees	often	far
never	run	Indians
started	important	really
city	until	almost
earth	children	let
eyes	side	above
light	feet	girl
thought	car	sometimes
head	miles	mountains
under	night	cut
story	walked	young
saw	white	talk
left	sea	soon
don't	began	list
few	grow	song
while	took	being
along	river	leave
might	four	family
close	carry	it's
something		

High-Frequency Words: Grades 4-5
Fry Instant Words

Grade 4

body	usually	hours
music	didn't	black
color	friends	products
stand	easy	happened
sun	heard	whole
questions	order	measure
fish	red	remember
area	door	early
mark	sure	waves
dog	become	reached
horse	top	listen
birds	ship	wind
problem	across	rock
complete	today	space
room	during	covered
knew	short	fast
since	better	several
ever	best	hold
piece	however	himself
told	low	toward

Grade 5

done	front	stay
English	feel	green
road	fact	known
halt	inches	island
ten	street	week
fly	decided	less
gave	contain	machine
box	course	base
finally	surface	ago
wait	produce	stood
correct	building	plane
oh	ocean	system
quickly	class	behind
personal	note	ran
became	nothing	round
shown	rest	boat
minutes	carefully	game
strong	scientists	force
verb	inside	brought
stars	wheels	understand

Comprehension Clues

When decoding a word:

- Look at the picture.
- Sound out the word. Does the word make sense in the sentence?
- Look for chunks, or smaller words, inside the word.
- Skip the word and then come back to it.
- Reread the word. Does it make sense in the sentence? If it doesn't, stop and go back.
- Find the word in a dictionary or thesaurus.
- Read ahead to gather more clues.

When decoding a passage:

- Think about what you already know about the topic.
- Make predictions about what might happen next in the story.
- Use context clues.
- Get information from any graphic features on the page.
- Review the chapter or section titles.
- Use organizational features, such as the index or the glossary.
- Restate what you've read in your own words.
- Review any notes you have taken.
- Think about the author's purpose.

Reading Comprehension Strategies

- Apply prior knowledge; make predictions.

- Visualize; create mental images.

- Monitor comprehension; repair understanding when the meaning breaks down.

- Determine the author's purpose.

- Recognize story elements.

- Sequence events; summarize.

- Identify the main idea and details.

- Determine important information.

- Generate questions; answer questions.

- Identify cause and effect.

- Make inferences.

- Draw conclusions.

- Evaluate; make judgments.

- Make connections: text to text; text to self; text to world.

- Use text structure and format.

- Use graphic organizers.

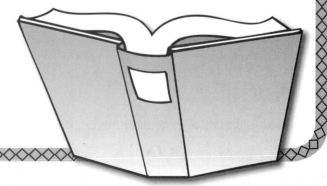

Genres

Fiction

first-person narrative
folklore
   fables
   legends
   myths
   tall tales
   trickster tales
historical fiction
humor
imaginative
   fairy tales
   fantasies
   fractured fairy tales
mystery
realistic fiction
science fiction
   environmental fiction
   fantasy

Nonfiction

autobiography
biography
informational
   articles
   letters
   texts
memoir

Poetry

Electronic Literacy

Literary Elements

Fiction

characters	plot
humor	setting
illustrations	theme
perspective	

Nonfiction

accuracy
author's purpose
characterization of subject
graphic features
illustrations
main ideas
organizational features
setting
structure
supporting details
text features
theme
vocabulary

Poetry

figurative language
meaning and emotion
rhyme and sound patterns
rhythm or cadence
shape

Electronic Literacy

graphics	on-screen text
hypertext	sound and vision
moving pictures	static pictures

Read-Aloud List: Grade One

Why Mosquitoes Buzz in People's Ears
Aardema, Verna

The Snail House
Ahlberg, Allan

My Friend Bear
Alborough, Jez

Parts
Arnold, Tedd

Dear Big, Mean, Ugly Monster
Berglin, Ruth M.

The Five Chinese Brothers
Bishop, Claire Huchet

Franklin Goes to School
Bourgeois, Paulette

Voices in the Park
Browne, Anthony

Arthur's Baby
Brown, Marc

Book! Book! Book!
Bruss, Deborah

The Little House
Burton, Virginia Lee

Boo's Dinosaur
Byars, Betsy

The Very Clumsy Click Beetle
Carle, Eric

I Like Me!
Carlson, Nancy

Just Another Ordinary Day
Clement, Rod

Starring First Grade
Cohen, Miriam

Miss Rumphius
Cooney, Barbara

Giggle, Giggle, Quack
Cronin, Doreen

Today I Feel Silly
Curtis, Jamie Lee

Strega Nona
dePaola, Tomie

Go Away, Big Green Monster
Emberley, Ed

Olivia Saves the Circus
Falconer, Ian

Koala Lou
Fox, Mem

Sheila Rae, the Brave
Henkes, Kevin

One Fine Day
Hogrogian, Nonny

Horace and Morris but Mostly Dolores
Howe, James

My Best Friend
Hutchins, Pat

The Incredible Book Eating Boy
Jeffers, Oliver

George Shrinks
Joyce, William

Leo the Late Bloomer
Kraus, Robert

I Wish That I Had Duck Feet
Le Sieg, Theo

Bats at the Beach
Lies, Brian

Fish Is Fish
Lionni, Leo

How I Became a Pirate
Long, Melinda

Stand Tall, Molly Lou Melon
Lovell, Patty

If You Give a Mouse a Cookie
Numeroff, Laura

Junie B. Jones and the Stupid Smelly Bus
Park, Barbara

Reading Makes You Feel Good
Parr, Todd

The Kissing Hand
Penn, Audrey

The Lion and the Mouse
Pinkney, Jerry

Ish
Reynolds, Peter H.

Rattletrap Car
Root, Phyllis

The Relatives Came
Rylant, Cynthia

Caps for Sale
Slobodkina, Esphyr

And the Dish Ran Away With the Spoon
Stevens, Janet

The Little Red Hen (Makes a Pizza)
Sturges, Philemon

Ira Sleeps Over
Waber, Bernard

There Is a Bird on Your Head
Willems, Mo

A Chair for My Mother
Williams, Vera B.

Owl Moon
Yolen, Jane

Read-Aloud List: Grades Two and Three

Miss Nelson Is Missing
Allard, Harry

The Indian in the Cupboard
Banks, Lynne Reid

Cloudy With a Chance of Meatballs
Barrett, Judi

Superfudge
Blume, Judy

The Mitten
Brett, Jan

Flat Stanley
Brown, Jeff

Fly Away Home
Bunting, Eve

The Stories Julian Tells
Cameron, Ann

Stellaluna
Cannon, Janell

The Mouse and the Motorcycle
Cleary, Beverly

Frindle
Clements, Andrew

Miss Rumphius
Cooney, Barbara

Jeremy Thatcher, Dragon Hatcher
Coville, Bruce

Click, Clack, Moo: Cows That Type
Cronin, Doreen

That's Good! That's Bad! In the Grand Canyon
Cuyler, Margery

Miss Alaineus: A Vocabulary Disaster
Frasier, Debra

Stone Fox
Gardiner, John Reynolds

Grandpa's Face
Greenfield, Eloise

Chet Gecko, Private Eye
Hale, Bruce

A Cache of Jewels
Heller, Ruth

The Year of Miss Agnes
Hill, Kirkpatrick

The Seven Silly Eaters
Hoberman, Mary Ann

Amazing Grace
Hoffman, Mary

Sweet Clara and the Freedom Quilt
Hopkinson, Deborah

Bunnicula
Howe, James

Class Clown
Hurwitz, Johanna

Anansi and the Talking Melon
Kimmel, Eric A.

Tacky the Penguin
Lester, Helen

Frog and Toad
Lobel, Arnold

Black and White
Macaulay, David

Mrs. Piggle-Wiggle
MacDonald, Betty

The Ghost-Eye Tree
Martin Jr., Bill, and John Archambault

The Plant That Ate Dirty Socks
McArthur, Nancy

Homer Price
McCloskey, Robert

Judy Moody
McDonald, Megan

Flossie and the Fox
McKissack, Patricia

Stephanie's Ponytail
Munsch, Robert

The Recess Queen
O'Neill, Alexis

The Keeping Quilt
Polacco, Patricia

How to Eat Fried Worms
Rockwell, Thomas

The True Story of the Three Little Pigs
Scieszka, Jon

The Sneetches and Other Stories
Seuss, Dr.

A Bad Case of Stripes
Shannon, David

Encyclopedia Brown
Sobol, Donald J.

Tops and Bottoms
Stevens, Janet

The Three Little Wolves and the Big Bad Pig
Trivizas, Eugene

Two Bad Ants
Van Allsburg, Chris

Chester
Watt, Melanie

Don't Let the Pigeon Drive the Bus
Willems, Mo

Lon Po Po
Young, Ed

Read-Aloud List: Grades Four and Five

The Lizard and the Sun
Ada, Alma Flor

Poppy
Avi

Tuck Everlasting
Babbitt, Natalie

Tales of a Fourth Grade Nothing
Blume, Judy

The Secret Garden
Burnett, Frances Hodgson

Wanted: Mud Blossom
Byars, Betsy

More Stories Julian Tells
Cameron, Ann

No Arm in Left Field
Christopher, Matt

Dear Mr. Henshaw
Cleary, Beverly

The School Story
Clements, Andrew

Bud Not Buddy
Curtis, Christopher Paul

The BFG
Dahl, Roald

Donavan's Word Jar
DeGross, Monalisa

Because of Winn-Dixie
DiCamillo, Kate

The Hundred Dresses
Estes, Eleanor

Julie
George, Jean Craighead

Old Yeller
Gipson, Fred

Honus and Me
Gutman, Dan

Faraway Summer
Hurwitz, Johanna

Paul Bunyan
Kellogg, Steven

From the Mixed-Up Files of Mrs. Basil E. Frankweiler
Konigsburg, E. L.

Catwings
Le Guin, Ursula K.

Pippi Longstocking
Lindgren, Astrid

Sarah, Plain and Tall
MacLachlan, Patricia

The Rough-Faced Girl
Martin, Rafe

Me, Mop, and the Moondance Kid
Myers, Walter Dean

Shiloh
Naylor, Phyllis Reynolds

If You Were a Writer
Nixon, Joan Lowery

The Borrowers
Norton, Mary

Mrs. Frisby and the Rats of NIMH
O'Brien, Robert C.

Skinnybones
Park, Barbara

The Great Gilly Hopkins
Paterson, Katherine

Cyrus the Unsinkable Sea Serpent
Peet, Bill

Something About Hensley's
Polacco, Patricia

The New Kid on the Block
Prelutsky, Jack

Percy Jackson and the Olympians
Riordan, Rick

The Best School Year Ever
Robinson, Barbara

The Absent Author
Roy, Ron

Holes
Sachar, Louis

The Stinky Cheese Man and Other Fairly Stupid Tales
Scieszka, Jon

The Lorax
Seuss, Dr.

A Light in the Attic
Silverstein, Shel

The Trading Game
Slote, Alfred

Maniac Magee
Spinelli, Jerry

Sylvester and the Magic Pebble
Steig, William

Roll of Thunder, Hear My Cry
Taylor, Mildred D.

Dicey's Song
Voight, Cynthia

Charlotte's Web
White, E. B.

Little House in the Big Woods
Wilder, Laura Ingalls

George Washington's Socks
Woodruff, Elvira

Compound Words

Two-Syllable Words

airplane
baseball
bedroom
birdhouse
birthday
bookcase
chalkboard
classmate
cowboy
crosswalk
daylight
downstairs
driveway
earring
earthquake
eggshell
fireplace
flagpole
football
goldfish
grapefruit
hairbrush
highway
hilltop
homework
indoor
keyboard
lifeguard
lighthouse
mailbox

nighttime
notebook
oatmeal
outside
paintbrush
pancake
peanut
playground
popcorn
railroad
rainbow
roadwork
sailboat
scarecrow
seashell
sidewalk
snowball
spaceship
staircase
starfish
suitcase
sunlight
teammate
toothbrush
touchdown
upstairs
warehouse
wheelchair
windmill
windshield

Three-Syllable Words

applesauce
basketball
butterfly
candlestick
everything
fingernail
flowerpot
gingerbread
grandfather
grandmother
grasshopper
hamburger
jellyfish
newspaper
nobody
rattlesnake
rollerblade
sandpaper
skyscraper
strawberry
underground
waterfall
woodpecker

Four-Syllable Words

anybody
everybody
motorcycle
underwater
videotape
watermelon

Contractions

am
I'm

is
here's
he's
it's
she's
that's
there's
what's
where's
who's

are
they're
we're
you're

not
aren't
can't
couldn't
didn't
doesn't
don't
hadn't
hasn't
haven't
isn't
mustn't
needn't
shouldn't
wouldn't

will
I'll
it'll
he'll
she'll
that'll
they'll
we'll
you'll

had/would
I'd
it'd
she'd
there'd
they'd
we'd
you'd

have
I've
they've
we've
you've

Synonyms

Synonyms are words that have the same or almost the same meaning.

afraid, frightened, scared	kind, considerate, thoughtful
after, later	leave, depart
anger, fury, rage	like, enjoy
back, rear	little, dinky, smallish
bad, naughty	looks, appears
begin, start	make, build, create, design
big, gigantic, huge, large	mean, cruel, nasty
brave, courageous, fearless	messy, sloppy
call, holler, shout, yell	neat, orderly, organized, tidy
close, shut	quiet, silent
cold, chilly, cool	rest, relax
cry, howl	say, tell
eat, consume	show, demonstrate, flaunt, guide
fast, quick	stop, halt, quit
fat, chubby	thin, slender
find, locate	think, imagine, ponder
fix, mend	under, below
happy, blissful, glad, joyous	use, apply
hold, grasp	wait, delay, postpone
hurt, injure	walk, stroll

The Ultimate Teacher's Book of Lists • ©The Mailbox® Books • TEC61339

Antonyms

Antonyms are words that have opposite or nearly opposite meanings.

above, below	day, night	in, out
absent, present	deep, shallow	join, separate
achieve, fail	defend, attack	kind, cruel
add, subtract	different, same	laugh, cry
admire, dislike	dirty, clean	lazy, energetic
admit, deny	down, up	left, right
all, none	dry, wet	long, short
allow, forbid	early, late	lose, win
answer, question	easy, difficult	multiply, divide
appear, vanish	empty, full	obey, command
arrive, depart	fancy, simple	on, off
asleep, awake	fast, slow	open, close
bad, good	fat, thin	over, under
beginning, end	find, lose	pain, pleasure
bent, straight	follow, lead	pass, fail
big, little	forget, remember	quiet, loud
blame, praise	friend, enemy	sick, healthy
bottom, top	front, back	simple, complex
boy, girl	give, take	start, finish
break, fix	go, stop	smooth, rough
bright, dull	hard, soft	sweet, bitter
build, take down	hate, like	true, false
cheap, expensive	help, hurt	ugly, attractive
come, go	high, low	young, old
danger, safety	hot, cold	

Homophones

Homophones are words that sound the same but have different meanings.

accept, except	grown, groan	right, write
ad, add	hair, hare	road, rode, rowed
aloud, allowed	hear, here	role, roll
ant, aunt	heard, herd	sail, sale
ate, eight	hi, high	sea, see
be, bee	hole, whole	sew, so, sow
bear, bare	hour, our	sight, site
blue, blew	idle, idol	some, sum
board, bored	its, it's	son, sun
break, brake	knew, new	stair, stare
capital, capitol	knot, not	steal, steel
cell, sell	knows, nose	suite, sweet
cent, scent	lessen, lesson	Sunday, sundae
cereal, serial	made, maid	tail, tale
chews, choose	mail, male	tea, tee
colonel, kernel	meat, meet	their, there, they're
dear, deer	one, won	threw, through
do, due, dew	pail, pale	throne, thrown
die, dye	pain, pane	to, too, two
fair, fare	pair, pare, pear	very, vary
fairy, ferry	patience, patients	wait, weight
feet, feat	pause, paws	wear, where, ware
flea, flee	peak, peek	weak, week
flew, flu	plain, plane	weather, whether
flower, flour	poor, pour, pore	which, witch
for, four, fore	principal, principle	who's, whose
forth, fourth	rap, wrap	wood, would
great, grate	red, read	your, you're

Multiple-Meaning Words

back	level	right
bank	load	roll
bat	map	ruler
bill	mean	second
block	note	shape
board	order	ship
color	pack	shovel
crash	paint	skate
cut	park	spot
draft	pet	spring
dress	picture	stalk
drill	pile	stamp
drop	place	string
eye	plane	swing
farm	plate	time
field	point	track
fire	pump	train
fish	puzzle	tune
float	racket	well
grade	raise	yard

Easily Confused Words

accept: agree to
except: leaving out

affect: influence
effect: outcome

all ready: prepared
already: before now

all together: at the same time, in the same place
altogether: all included

anyway: at least
any way: whichever method

apart: not together
a part: a piece

bibliography: list of books and articles on a subject
biography: book about a person's life

can: be able to
may: have permission to

command: order
commend: praise

council: committee
counsel: advise

desert: land that receives little rainfall
dessert: sweet eaten at the end of a meal

farther: at a greater distance
further: extra, additional

finally: at last
finely: keenly, in small pieces

good: favorable (an adjective, used to describe nouns)
well: in a good manner (an adverb, used to modify verbs)

its: belonging to it
it's: *it is* or *it has*

lay: put (something) down
lie: stretch out

leave: go away from
let: allow

passed: went by or beyond
past: history

peak: highest point
peek: glance

personal: private
personnel: workers

picture: drawing, painting, or photograph
pitcher: baseball player who throws the ball to the batter

principal: leader
principle: rule, law

rather: somewhat
whether: either

set: place something
sit: be seated

supposed to: obligated to
suppose: believe

sweet: sugary
suite: connected rooms

than: compared to
then: after that

thorough: complete
through: from end to end

who: person performing the action of the verb (a subject)
whom: person to whom the action is being done (an object)

who's: *who is* or *who has*
whose: belonging to whom

Prefixes

Prefix	Meaning	Example
anti-	against	antisocial
de-	opposite of, down	depart
dis-	not, opposite of	disagree
em-, en-	cause to	embody, enjoy
fore-	before	foreground
ill-, im-, in-, ir-	not, opposite of	illegal, impossible, indirect, irregular
im-, in-	not	impractical, inactive
inter-	between, among	interact
mid-	middle	midsummer
mis-	wrongly	misspell
non-	not, opposite of	nonfiction
over-	too much, above	overdress
pre-	before	prepay
re-	again, back	rewrite
semi-	half	semicircle
sub-	under, lower	subsoil
super-	above, beyond	supermarket
trans-	across	transport
un-	not, opposite of	unpack
under-	too little, below	underfed

Suffixes

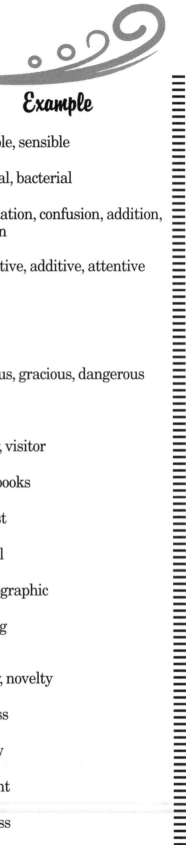

Suffix	Meaning	Example
-able, -ible	can be done	enjoyable, sensible
-al, -ial	having characteristics of	electrical, bacterial
-ation, -ion, -ition, -tion	act, process	continuation, confusion, addition, affection
-ative, -itive, -ive	of or related to	affirmative, additive, attentive
-ed	used to form past-tense verbs	walked
-en	made of	golden
-eous, -ious, -ous	possessing the qualities of	nauseous, gracious, dangerous
-er	used to form a comparative word	longer
-er, -or	one who	teacher, visitor
-es, -s	used to form plurals	boxes, books
-est	most	smallest
-ful	full of	truthful
-ic	having characteristics of	autobiographic
-ing	used to show a verb form or present participle	learning
-ity, -ty	state of	lucidity, novelty
-less	without	priceless
-ly	characteristic of	friendly
-ment	action or process	payment
-ness	state of, condition of	kindness
-y	characterized by	sticky

Greek and Latin Roots

Greek Word Roots

Root	Meaning	Example	Root	Meaning	Example
aer	air	aerial	logo	word, reason	logogram
agog	leader	synagogue	meter/metr	measure	perimeter, metric
angel	messenger	angelic	micro	small	microscope
aster/astr	star	asterisk, astrology	mono	one, single	monotone
			od/hod	road, way	episode, method
auto	self	autobiography	phe/phem	to speak	hyphen, grapheme
bio	life	biology	phil	love	philosophy
chlor	greenish-yellow	chlorine	phon	sound	telephone
chron	time	chronicle	phos/photo	light	phosphorus, photograph
derm	skin	dermatology	pol/polis	city, state	police, metropolis
eco	house	ecology	scope	instrument for viewing	microscope
gram	thing, written	telegram			
graph	writing	autograph	techn	art, skill, craft	technology
hydr	water	hydrant	therm	heat	thermometer
hyper	over, above, beyond	hypercritical	zoo	animal	zoology
hypo	below, beneath	hypodermis			

Latin Word Roots

Root	Meaning	Example	Root	Meaning	Example
aud	to hear	audio	rupt	to break	disrupt
bene	well, good	beneficial	scrib/script	to write	describe, transcript
cred	to believe, to trust	credit	sec/sect	cut	second, insect
dict	to say	dictate	spect	to look	to inspect
duc(t)	to lead	product	spir	to breathe	respiration
fac	to do, to make	factory	struct	to build	construct
flec/flex	to bend	reflect, flexible	st/sta/stat	to stand	arrest, stable, station
form	shape	formula	tact/tang	to touch	contact, tangible
fract	to break	fraction	trac/tract	to drag, pull	trace, tractor
ject	throw	object	vers/vert	to turn	inverse, revert
jud	judge	judgment	vid/vis	to see	video, television
junct	to join	junction	voc	voice, to call	vocal
port	to carry	portable	vor	eat	omnivore

Greek and Latin Affixes

Greek Prefixes

Prefix	Meaning
a-, an-	without
anti-, ant-	opposite
auto-	self, same
bio-, bi-	life, living organism
geo-	Earth
hyper-	excessive
micro-	small
mono-	one, single, alone
neo-	new, recent
pan-	all
thermo-, therm-	heat

Greek Suffixes

Suffix	Meaning
-ist	one that does
-ism	act, state, or theory of
-graph	instrument for writing, drawing, or recording
-gram	something written or drawn
-log, -logue	speech, discourse
-logy	discourse, study
-meter, -metry	measuring device
-oid	like, resembling; shape, form
-phile	one that loves
-phobe, -phobia	one that fears a specific thing
-phone	sound

Latin Prefixes

Prefix	Meaning
co-	together
de-	away, off
dis-	not, not any
inter-	between, among
non-	not
post-	after
pre-	before
re-	again; back
sub-	under
trans-	across, beyond, through

Latin Suffixes

Suffix	Meaning
-able, -ible	capable or worthy of
-ation	forms nouns from verbs
-ify, -fy	to make or cause to become
-ity, -ty	forms nouns from adjectives
-ment	forms nouns from verbs

Multisyllable Words

Three-Syllable Words	Four-Syllable Words	Five-Syllable Words
adventure	absolutely	alliteration
banana	activity	auditorium
bicycle	adorable	certification
butterfly	alligator	communication
caravan	calculator	congratulations
crocodile	caterpillar	contemporary
difficult	conversation	creativity
elephant	dependable	dermatologist
factory	energetic	electricity
fantastic	enjoyable	hippopotamus
gigantic	escalator	humidifier
habitat	exaggerate	nutritionally
invention	hysterical	opportunity
kangaroo	independent	organization
magical	information	pediatrician
marshmallow	kindergarten	pronunciation
mosquito	magnificent	qualification
multiply	material	representative
pineapple	motorcycle	unacceptable
poisonous	mysterious	unbelievable
popular	operation	undergraduate
strawberry	pepperoni	university
tornado	population	unnecessary
vacation	tarantula	vegetarian
wonderful	watermelon	vocabulary

Nouns and Pronouns

A **noun** is a word that names a person, place, thing, or idea. A **pronoun** is a word that takes the place of a noun.

Nouns

Person	Place	Thing	Idea
astronaut	backyard	bicycle	friendship
baby	beach	book	happiness
carpenter	building	calendar	joy
doctor	city	car	love
farmer	country	computer	sadness
friend	desert	dragon	trouble
lawyer	farm	guitar	
librarian	garage	health	
mayor	garden	homework	
neighbor	home	magazine	
nurse	island	pollution	
parent	jungle	race	
passenger	library	reward	
principal	park	scent	
stranger	railway	squirrel	
student	restaurant	temper	
teacher	school	wealth	
veterinarian	wilderness	weather	

Pronouns

Singular		Plural	
he	me	our	us
her	mine	ours	we
hers	my	their	you
him	our	theirs	your
his	she	them	yours
I	you	they	
it	your		
its	yours		

Verbs

Action Verbs

An **action verb** is a word that tells what the subject is doing.

ask	drop	march	run
bake	dust	mark	sail
bite	eat	meet	scream
blow	float	melt	shop
call	fly	paint	skate
chase	grab	pick	smile
cheer	greet	plant	speak
chew	grin	play	sweep
chop	guess	point	swim
climb	hope	pull	swing
come	hug	push	talk
cook	hunt	race	throw
drag	jog	read	wash
drink	jump	ride	win
drive	keep	roll	write

Linking Verbs

A **linking verb** links the subject and the predicate.

am	are	be	been	is	was	were

Helping Verbs

A **helping verb** comes before the main verb and helps tell an action or show time.

am	did	is	was
are	do	may	were
been	had	must	will
can	has	shall	
could	have	should	

Adjectives

An **adjective** is a word that describes a noun or pronoun.

adorable	difficult	kind
aggressive	disgusted	lazy
alert	eager	lonely
angry	easy	long
annoyed	energetic	lucky
attractive	enthusiastic	magnificent
awful	evil	mysterious
bad	excited	naughty
beautiful	expensive	odd
bored	famous	perfect
brainy	fancy	poor
brave	fantastic	powerful
bright	fierce	precious
busy	filthy	proud
calm	foolish	rich
careful	friendly	scary
cautious	frightened	selfish
cheerful	funny	shiny
clever	gentle	shy
clumsy	gorgeous	silly
colorful	graceful	strange
confused	grumpy	talented
cooperative	handsome	terrible
courageous	happy	thoughtful
cruel	helpful	tired
curious	hilarious	tough
cute	horrible	unusual
dangerous	hungry	wicked
dark	jealous	wild
delightful	jolly	worried

Other adjectives are **color words, quantity words, shape words,** and **size words.**
Adjectives also include the following **articles:** a, an, the.

Adverbs

An **adverb** adds meaning to a verb, adjective, or another adverb.
Adverbs usually tell how, where, or when.

Adverbs of time tell when an action happens.

afterwards	immediately	repeatedly
always	instantly	seldom
annually	monthly	sometimes
continually	never	soon
daily	now	tomorrow
early	often	usually
eventually	promptly	weekly
first	rarely	yearly
hourly	regularly	yesterday

Adverbs of manner tell how something is done.

accidentally	fairly	neatly
almost	fast	openly
angrily	gently	partially
badly	gladly	perfectly
beautifully	greatly	quickly
bravely	happily	quietly
busily	hungrily	restfully
calmly	joyfully	sadly
carefully	kindly	silently
closely	less	successfully
delightfully	likely	terribly
easily	loudly	truly
even	more	very
excitedly	nearly	warmly

Adverbs of place tell where something occurs.

everywhere	nearby
far	there
here	outside
inside	

Prepositions

A **preposition** is a word that relates the noun or pronoun in a sentence to another word. A **prepositional phrase** is a group of words that includes the preposition followed by a noun or pronoun.

aboard	by	out of
about	down	over
above	during	past
across	except	since
after	for	through
against	from	throughout
along	in	till
alongside	in front of	to
among	inside	toward
around	into	under
at	like	underneath
before	near	until
behind	of	unto
below	off	up
beneath	on	upon
beside	onto	with
between	on top of	within
beyond	out	without

Conjunctions and Interjections

A **conjunction** is a word or phrase that connects words or groups of words together.

after	for	though
although	if	unless
and	in order that	until
as	nor	when
as if	or	where
because	since	while
before	so	yet
but	that	

An **interjection** is a word or phrase that is used to tell strong emotion, such as anger, surprise, pain, or relief. A comma or an exclamation mark is used after the interjection.

golly	oh my	wow
goodness	oops	yeah
ha-ha	ouch	yes
hey	stop	yippee
hooray	uh-oh	yuck
oh	what	

Developmental Stages

Spelling Stages

Preschool to middle of grade 1 (Emergent Stage)

Early Emergent: writes on the page, draws and scribbles, no directionality, no sound-symbol correspondence

Middle Emergent: distinct writing and drawing; lines and dots for writing; letter-like forms; confuses letters, numbers, and letter-like forms; may wrap writing from right to left at end of line; no sound-symbol correspondence

Late Emergent: consistent directionality; some letter-sound correspondence; substitutes letters that sound, feel, and look alike; incomplete sound-symbol correspondence; inconsistent spacing between words

Kindergarten to middle of grade 2 (Letter Name–Alphabetic Stage)

Early: represents most prominent sounds, correct directionality, writes most letters of the alphabet, clear letter-sound correspondence, partially spells consonant blends and digraphs, confuses some letters, often confuses long vowels, beginning and end of syllables is inconsistent, leaves out spacing between some words, leaves out vowels in syllables

Middle: spells most beginning and ending consonants, clear letter-sound correspondence, correctly spells frequently occurring short-vowel words, confuses letter names in short vowels, confuses some consonant blends and digraphs

Late: spells regular short-vowel patterns, spells most consonant blends and digraphs, spells some common long-vowel words, substitutes common patterns for low-frequency short vowels, misspells most long-vowel markers or silent vowels, leaves out vowels in unstressed syllables

Grade 1 to middle of Grade 4 (Within Word Pattern Stage)

Early: spells initial, final consonants; spells consonant blends, digraphs; spells regular short-vowel patterns; accuracy on *r*-controlled single-syllable words; spells some infrequently used short-vowel and frequently used long-vowel words; confuses long-vowel markers; does not double consonants (for *hop*, spells *hoping* for *hopping*); does not use vowels in unaccented syllables

Middle: spells over half of the long-vowel words in single-syllable words; confuses long-vowel markers; confuses consonant patterns; confuses frequent, unstressed syllable patterns; confuses common inflections

Late: spells single-syllable long-vowel words; knows some common Latin suffixes, spells some phonetically; confuses low-frequency long-vowel words; confuses common inflections; does not double consonants; does not drop silent *e*

Developmental Stages

Grades 3 to 8 (Syllables and Affixes Stage)

Early: spells initial, final consonants; spells consonant blends, digraphs; short-vowel patterns; most long-vowel patterns; most inflections; confuses consonant doubling; confuses long-vowel patterns in accented syllables; confuses reduced vowel in unaccented syllables; confuses doubling and drops silent *e*; occasionally deletes middle syllables

Middle: spells consonant doubles, correctly doubles consonants and drops silent *e*, confuses less-stressed syllables, spells sounds at syllable junctures like single-syllable words, does not spell assimilated prefixes, does not consistently spell roots

Late: spells long-vowel patterns in accented syllables, doubles consonants and drops silent *e*, confuses some suffixes and prefixes, confuses vowel alternation, confuses consonant alternation

Grades 5 to 12 (Derivational Relations Stage)

Early: spells most words, spells most vowel and consonant alternations, misspells unaccented or *schwa* sounds, confuses some silent consonants, confuses some consonant doubling, confuses some suffixes and prefixes, confuses some vowel alternations, does not spell silent letters related to derivation

Middle: spells most words, spells common Latin suffixes, confuses some silent letters, misspells some reduced vowels

Late: spells most words, confuses assimilated prefixes, confuses unfamiliar derived forms, misspells some uncommon roots

Writing Stages

Emergent Preschool to middle of grade 1	**Beginning** Kindergarten to middle of grade 2	**Transitional** Grade 1 to middle of grade 4	**Intermediate** Grades 3 to 8
✓ pretend writing	✓ word-by-word writing that may include writing a few words or lines	✓ writing approaches fluency ✓ more organized ✓ may write several paragraphs	✓ writing fluently with expression and voice ✓ writing with different styles in different genres ✓ shows personal problem solving and reflection

Abbreviations and Transition Words

Abbreviations

Metric Capacity
milliliter = mL
centiliter = cL
deciliter = dL
liter = L
kiloliter = kL

Metric Length
millimeter = mm
centimeter = cm
decimeter = dm
meter = m
kilometer = km

Metric Weight
milligram = mg
centigram = cg
decigram = dg
gram = g
kilogram = kg

Standard Capacity
cup = c.
pint = pt.
quart = qt.
gallon = gal.

Standard Length
inch = in.
foot = ft.
yard = yd.
mile = mi.

Standard Weight
ounce = oz.
pound = lb.
ton = T

Months
January = Jan.
February = Feb.
March = Mar.
April = Apr.
May = May
June = Jun.
July = Jul.
August = Aug.
September = Sept.
October = Oct.
November = Nov.
December = Dec.

Places
Avenue = Ave.
Boulevard = Blvd.
Drive = Dr.
Highway = Hwy.
Road = Rd.
Street = St.
East = E.
North = N.
South = S.
West = W.

Transitions

Location
above   in front of
behind   into
below   near

Time
as soon as   second
before   soon
during   today
first   tomorrow
later   until

Compare two things
as   like
also

Contrast things
although   even though
but   however

Emphasize a point
a fact   for this reason
again

Add information
also   as well
and   besides
another   for example

Conclude, summarize
finally   in conclusion
lastly   in summary

Plural Words

Add *s* to most words.

Singular	Plural
desk	desks
map	maps
snake	snakes

Add *es* to words that end in *ch, s, sh, x,* or *z*.

Singular	Plural
box	boxes
brush	brushes
buzz	buzzes
glass	glasses
peach	peaches
witch	witches

Change *y* to *i*. Add *es*.

Singular	Plural
baby	babies
fly	flies
sky	skies

There are some exceptions to this rule, such as words that end in a vowel plus *y*.

Singular	Plural
jay	jays
toy	toys
turkey	turkeys

Add *es* or *s* to words that end in *o*.

Singular	Plural
hero	heroes
potato	potatoes
tomato	tomatoes
piano	pianos
radio	radios
taco	tacos

There are some exceptions to this rule, such as words that can be spelled with *es* or *s*.

Singular	Plural
banjo	banjo(e)s
lasso	lasso(e)s
zero	zero(e)s

Change *f* to *v*. Add *es*.

Singular	Plural
life	lives
scarf	scarves
self	selves

Some words have the same singular and plural form.

Singular	Plural
deer	deer
moose	moose
sheep	sheep

Irregular Plurals

Singular	Plural	Singular	Plural
child	children	man	men
die	dice	mouse	mice
foot	feet	ox	oxen
goose	geese	person	people
louse	lice	woman	women

Open-Syllable Words and Closed-Syllable Words

Words With an Open First Syllable

able	double	model	robot
apron	eagle	modem	rosy
baby	even	music	sofa
basic	final	notice	spider
beaver	flavor	open	student
begin	future	paper	super
belong	habit	pilot	table
beyond	hotel	polar	tiger
bible	label	prepare	tiny
bonus	lava	program	trouble
cable	legal	relax	truly
depend	locate	reward	unit

Words With a Closed First Syllable

album	desert	napkin	subject
absent	explain	object	subtract
basket	fabric	olive	sudden
cabin	finish	onto	sunlamp
campus	happen	pencil	talent
candle	imprint	pilgrim	tremble
combat	indeed	plaster	turtle
comet	insect	pulpit	under
confuse	insult	pumpkin	unzip
consult	kitten	rabbit	velvet
contest	lemon	spinach	weaken
dentist	mishap	stumble	wrinkle

Overused Words and Phrases

Tired Word or Phrase	Suggestions for Replacements	Tired Word or Phrase	Suggestions for Replacements
all	entire, whole	lots	bunches, heaps
a lot	much, often	mad	angry, frustrated
also	as well as, in addition to	next	after that, subsequently
any	several, some	nice	delightful, pleasant
awesome	fantastic, wonderful	pretty	attractive, fetching
awful	frightful, terrible	ran	hurried, rushed
beautiful	gorgeous, striking	sad	downcast, sorrowful
begin	embark on, set in motion	said	declared, repeated
better	enhanced, improved	saw	eyed, glimpsed
big	mammoth, towering	scared	fearful, terrified
book	text, work	see/saw	observe, witness
boring	repetitive, tiresome	seem	appear, give the impression
but	however, still	short	low-lying, pint-size
cool	amazing, remarkable	sick	ill, unwell
end	conclusion, finish	since	because, in view of the fact that
fun	amusing, entertaining		
funny	humorous, laughable	smart	clever, ingenious
get/got	obtained, received	smile	beam, grin
go	move, travel	so	thus, therefore
good	decent, reasonable	stuff	article, materials
great	marvelous, wonderful	suddenly	abruptly, out of the blue
guy	boy, fellow	terrific	bang-up, top-notch
happy	cheerful, pleased	then	later, second
have to	must, need to	things	objects, substance
kid	child, youngster	totally	completely, entirely
kind of	more or less, sort of	try	attempt, undertake
laughed	giggled, snickered	very	incredibly, truly
like	care for, similar	walked	hiked, strolled
little	miniature, slight	watch	inspect, survey
		well	fit, healthy

Writing Terms

audience: the people a story is written for

body: the main part of the writing that follows the introduction and comes before the closing

brainstorming: planning for writing by gathering ideas and information

caption: a description of a picture or photograph in a piece of writing

characters: the people or animals in a story

conclusion: the end of a story

description: writing to clearly describe a person, place, thing, or idea

editing: checking spelling, grammar, and mechanics; also checking for clear writing

form: the type of writing, such as a story, play, poem, or essay

grammar: the rules of language in writing and speaking

main idea: the central theme of a writing project

narrator: the one telling a story

novel: a fictional book

personal narrative: writing to tell a story from your own life

personification: a figure of speech in which an object or animal is given qualities of a person

plot: what happens in a story

prewriting: planning before writing

proofreading: checking the final draft of a writing for spelling, grammar, and mechanics

revising: making changes to a draft to improve it

sensory details: words or phrases used to describe how something looks, feels, sounds, smells, or tastes

setting: when and where the story takes place

supporting details: details used to support the main idea

topic: the main subject in a writing project

voice: the manner in which a writer expresses ideas

Proofreader Marks

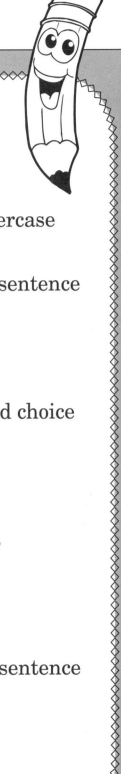

cap (b̲)	capitalization
⌄	add comma
⊙	add period
⌄ ⌄	add quotation marks
∧	add
⌄	add apostrophe
⊙	add colon
¶	indent paragraph
ℒ	delete
#	insert a space

frag.	fragment
lc ℬ	make lowercase
ram.	rambling sentence
sp.	spell out
w.c.	check word choice
n.c.	not clear
⬭	check this
wordy	too wordy
TS	add topic sentence

Spelling and Writing

Types of Writing

---

descriptive: writing to describe a subject; incorporates sensory details and vivid images

advertisement	comic	movie review
autobiography	diary entry	newspaper article
award	informational article	poem
biography	instructions	riddle
book review	journal entry	song
cartoon	letter	summary

---

expository: writing to inform or explain a subject

advertisement	informational article	newspaper article
biography	instructions	report
book review	job application	research paper
diary entry	journal entry	song
essay	letter	speech
how-to article	movie review	summary

---

narrative: writing to tell a story; fact or fiction

autobiography	fairy tale	play
biography	folktale	poem
cartoon	joke	script (movie, play, TV show)
comic strip	journal entry	
diary entry	letter (congratulations, friendly)	song
essay		tall tale
fable	movie review	

---

persuasive: writing to state an opinion and persuade the reader to agree

advertisement	joke	newspaper article
advice column	journal entry	resumé
book review	letter (complaint, job application, letter to the editor)	slogan
diary entry		song
editorial		speech
essay	movie review	

Types of Poetry

acrostic: a word is spelled vertically; each letter begins a line of the poem

alphabet: each line of the poem begins with a different letter in alphabetic order

ballad: tells a short story; it is written in stanzas of four lines in which the second and fourth lines often rhyme

cinquain: five-line poem; each line has a specific number of syllables

     title (two syllables)
     description of title (four syllables)
     action about title (six syllables)
     feeling about title (eight syllables)
     synonym for title (two syllables)

couplet: two-line verse that usually rhymes

free verse: does not follow a specific form; does not have to rhyme

haiku: three-line poem usually about nature; first line is five syllables, second line is seven syllables, and third line is five syllables

limerick: five-line poem that involves humor; lines one, two, and five rhyme and lines three and four rhyme

lyric: uses sensory details to tell about a person's emotions; often written like a song

quatrain: four-line poem or stanza; often alternate lines rhyme

triplet: three-line verse that usually rhymes

Story Parts

antagonist: the character who is fighting against the hero

character: person or animal in a story

climax: a turning point in the action

conflict: the main problem; can occur between two or more characters or between a character and himself, society, nature, or the supernatural

mood: the feeling the reader gets from reading a story

narrator: the person telling a story

plot: the events and actions that take a story from the beginning to the end

protagonist: the hero in a story

setting: when and where a story takes place

theme: the story's message or subject

Writing Process

Prewriting: Select a main idea for the story. Plan the characters, setting, problem/solution, events, and details.
   Suggested activities:
   - brainstorming
   - researching
   - using a graphic organizer
   - interviewing
   - writing an outline
   - illustrating
   - talking with a partner

First Draft: Write the story to get all your ideas on paper. Refer to your prewriting as a guide.

Revising: Make changes to improve your draft. Add or delete ideas.
   Suggested activities:
   - Reread your story twice.
   - Have a classmate read your story and provide feedback.
   - Rearrange details.
   - Clarify.

Editing and proofreading: Make final changes to make writing clear and accurate. Look for content and mechanics (spelling, grammar, punctuation, and capitalization).

Publishing: Share the story with others by reading it aloud or posting it for others to read.

Sensory Words

Sound Words

barking	chirping	crying	rustling
bawling	clicking	gagging	slamming
booming	cooing	grunting	snoring
buzzing	coughing	laughing	thumping
chattering	crunching	ringing	whispering

Sight Words

blushing	crinkled	gleaming	shaggy
bright	filthy	luminous	shimmering
bulky	fluffy	motionless	sloppy
clean	gigantic	murky	spotless
colorful	glassy	radiant	unsightly

Taste Words

acidic	hot	salty	sweet
bitter	minty	savory	tangy
bland	nutty	sour	tart
creamy	peppery	spicy	
delicious	ripe	stale	

Smell Words

bitter	fragrant	rancid	spicy
burnt	fresh	rotten	stale
clean	medicinal	salty	stinky
delicious	musty	smoky	strong
flowery	pungent	sour	sweet

Touch Words

bumpy	gooey	leathery	slippery
chilly	greasy	prickly	sticky
damp	gritty	searing	tender
dry	hairy	sharp	uneven
fluffy	heavy	silky	velvety

Feeling Words

Anger
annoyed
bitter
bugged
crabby
cranky
furious
grouchy
irate
sore
spiteful

Caring
adoring
affectionate
considerate
devoted
fond of
friendly
kind
like
respecting
wild about

Confusion
bewildered
distracted
foggy
mistaken
puzzled
rattled
reeling
shocked
shook-up
speechless

Fear
afraid
alarmed
anxious
fearful
frightened
horrified
jumpy
nervous
shocked
tense

Happiness
aglow
contented
delighted
ecstatic
gleeful
light-hearted
overjoyed
satisfied
thrilled
tickled pink

Hurt/Lonely
aching
crushed
cut off
detached
disgraced
oppressed
outcast
put down
rejected
withdrawn

Regretful
apologetic
ashamed
demeaned
embarrassed
guilty
hesitant
humiliated
remorseful
sorrowful
sorry

Sadness
blue
dejected
depressed
downcast
empty
grim
lost
moody
tearful
worried

Miscellaneous
bored
curious
enthralled
greedy
homesick
hopeful
insecure
insulted
jealous
pessimistic

Noisy Words

Onomatopoeic words sound like the things they describe.

Arf!

baa	crunch	murmur	snarl
bang	cuckoo	mutter	sniff
bark	ding-dong	neigh	snort
beep	drip	oink	splash
belch	eek	ping	splat
bonk	fizz	pitter-patter	splatter
boo	fizzle	plop	squawk
boom	flick	plunk	squeak
burp	groan	poof	squish
buzz	growl	pop	thud
cackle	grunt	purr	thump
caw	gurgle	quack	tick-tock
chirp	hack	rattle	tweet
clang	hiccup	ribbit	whack
clank	hiss	roar	wham
clap	honk	rumble	whirr
clatter	howl	rustle	whiz
click	hum	screech	whoosh
clip-clop	knock-knock	shush	woof
clunk	meow	sizzle	yap
crackle	moan	slurp	yelp
creak	moo	smack	zing
croak	mumble	snap	zip

Zoom!

Idioms

an expression made of two or more words that together mean something other than the words' literal meanings

add fuel to the fire
all ears
at the end of your rope
back to square one
bells and whistles
busy as a beaver
butterflies in your stomach
climbing the walls
cold feet
down in the dumps
dull as dishwater
easy as pie
eat your words
feel your oats
fit as a fiddle
fly off the handle
get real
get your feet wet
go bananas
hanging by a thread

hit the books
in the bag
in the pink
jump the gun
kill two birds with
    one stone
knock on wood
leave no stone unturned
let sleeping dogs lie

like two peas in a pod
make waves
mind over matter
needle in a haystack
on cloud nine
out on a limb
over your head
pass the buck

piece of cake
pull yourself together
put your foot down
quiet as a mouse
raining cats and dogs
red tape
saved by the bell
sink or swim
sitting pretty
take a backseat
throw in the towel
tickled pink
tip of the iceberg
turn the other cheek
under the weather
walking on eggshells
wet blanket
word of mouth
you can't teach an old
    dog new tricks

Alliterative Words and Phrases

repeating the same beginning sound in two or more neighboring words or syllables

active alligators
boys' books
chewy cherries

droopy dragons
extraordinary eggs
flashy flowers

pointed pencils
ugly umbrellas
wagon wheels

Many men munch on mulberry muffins in the morning.
Sue served six sodas and salads to her smiling sisters.
Two tiny toucans tasted tart tangerines while they tickled
    their tail feathers in the treetops.

Similes

making a comparison using *like* or *as*

Similes that use *as*

as blind as a bat
as clean as a whistle
as cold as ice
as cool as a cucumber
as cute as a button
as dark as night
as dead as a doornail
as dry as a bone
as fresh as a daisy
as gentle as a lamb
as good as gold
as hard as a rock
as light as a feather
as mad as a hornet
as sick as a dog
as straight as an arrow

as sturdy as an oak
as thin as a rake
as white as a ghost
as wise as an owl

Similes that use *like*

chattering like monkeys
cry like a baby
eats like a bird
eyes like a hawk
fits like a glove
fight like cats and dogs
glistens like dewdrops
moves like a snail

roars like a lion
runs like a deer
shines like stars
sings like an angel
sits like a bump on a log
slept like a log
smells like a rose
soar like an eagle
stands out like a sore thumb
swims like a fish
work like a dog
works like a charm

Metaphors

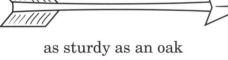

comparing two different things without using a comparison word

All the world's a stage.
The assignment was a breeze.
A blanket of snow covered the house.
The full moon is a perfect saucer.
She has the heart of a lion.
He has a heart of gold.
Our legs turned to rubber.
Her light curly hair is a golden crown.

Our town is a melting pot.
The news is music to her ears.
The plans are rock solid.
The road was a ribbon threading
through the hills.
We were swimming in a sea of
diamonds.
You're the apple of my eye.

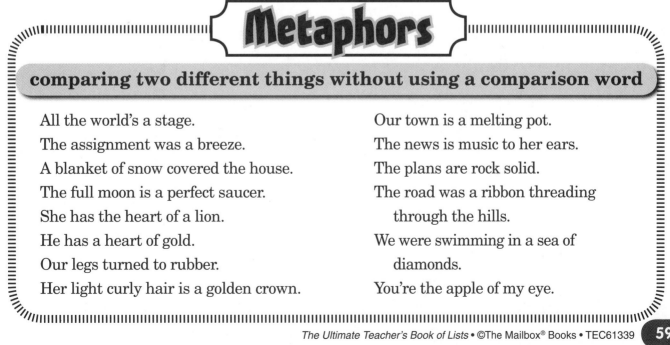

Addition Facts

0 + 0 = 0	0 + 1 = 1	0 + 2 = 2	0 + 3 = 3	0 + 4 = 4
1 + 0 = 1	1 + 1 = 2	1 + 2 = 3	1 + 3 = 4	1 + 4 = 5
2 + 0 = 2	2 + 1 = 3	2 + 2 = 4	2 + 3 = 5	2 + 4 = 6
3 + 0 = 3	3 + 1 = 4	3 + 2 = 5	3 + 3 = 6	3 + 4 = 7
4 + 0 = 4	4 + 1 = 5	4 + 2 = 6	4 + 3 = 7	4 + 4 = 8
5 + 0 = 5	5 + 1 = 6	5 + 2 = 7	5 + 3 = 8	5 + 4 = 9
6 + 0 = 6	6 + 1 = 7	6 + 2 = 8	6 + 3 = 9	6 + 4 = 10
7 + 0 = 7	7 + 1 = 8	7 + 2 = 9	7 + 3 = 10	7 + 4 = 11
8 + 0 = 8	8 + 1 = 9	8 + 2 = 10	8 + 3 = 11	8 + 4 = 12
9 + 0 = 9	9 + 1 = 10	9 + 2 = 11	9 + 3 = 12	9 + 4 = 13
10 + 0 = 10	10 + 1 = 11	10 + 2 = 12	10 + 3 = 13	10 + 4 = 14

0 + 5 = 5	0 + 6 = 6	0 + 7 = 7	0 + 8 = 8	0 + 9 = 9
1 + 5 = 6	1 + 6 = 7	1 + 7 = 8	1 + 8 = 9	1 + 9 = 10
2 + 5 = 7	2 + 6 = 8	2 + 7 = 9	2 + 8 = 10	2 + 9 = 11
3 + 5 = 8	3 + 6 = 9	3 + 7 = 10	3 + 8 = 11	3 + 9 = 12
4 + 5 = 9	4 + 6 = 10	4 + 7 = 11	4 + 8 = 12	4 + 9 = 13
5 + 5 = 10	5 + 6 = 11	5 + 7 = 12	5 + 8 = 13	5 + 9 = 14
6 + 5 = 11	6 + 6 = 12	6 + 7 = 13	6 + 8 = 14	6 + 9 = 15
7 + 5 = 12	7 + 6 = 13	7 + 7 = 14	7 + 8 = 15	7 + 9 = 16
8 + 5 = 13	8 + 6 = 14	8 + 7 = 15	8 + 8 = 16	8 + 9 = 17
9 + 5 = 14	9 + 6 = 15	9 + 7 = 16	9 + 8 = 17	9 + 9 = 18
10 + 5 = 15	10 + 6 = 16	10 + 7 = 17	10 + 8 = 18	10 + 9 = 19

	Doubles
0 + 10 = 10	
1 + 10 = 11	1 + 1 = 2
2 + 10 = 12	2 + 2 = 4
3 + 10 = 13	3 + 3 = 6
4 + 10 = 14	4 + 4 = 8
5 + 10 = 15	5 + 5 = 10
6 + 10 = 16	6 + 6 = 12
7 + 10 = 17	7 + 7 = 14
8 + 10 = 18	8 + 8 = 16
9 + 10 = 19	9 + 9 = 18
10 + 10 = 20	10 + 10 = 20

Addition Strategies

Count on.
Begin with the larger number and count on.

$$3 + 9 = ?$$

Think: 9, 10, 11, 12
    1 2 3

Use near doubles.
Change the problem to the closest doubles fact and then count on.

$$7 + 8 = ?$$

Think: $7 + 7 = 14$
   $14 + 1 = 15$

$$7 + 8 = 15$$

Make ten.
Change the problem to find the sum of 10 and then count on.

$$6 + 7 = ?$$

Think: $6 + 4 = 10$
   $10 + 3 = 13$

$$6 + 7 = 13$$

Add the places.
Change one addend into smaller place values and then add.

$$56 + 34 = ?$$

Think: $56 + 30 = 86$
   $86 + 4 = 90$

$$56 + 34 = 90$$

Add tens.
Change one addend into tens and ones and then add.

$$36 + 42 = ?$$

Think:
$$36$$
$$10 > 46$$
$$10 > 56$$
$$10 > 66$$
$$10 > 76$$
$$+\ 2$$
$$\overline{78}$$

$$36 + 42 = 78$$

Bridge to tens.
Add up to a multiple of ten and then add on.

$$17 + 6 = ?$$

Think: $17 + 3 = 20$
   $20 + 3 = 23$

$$17 + 6 = 23$$

Round.
Round the numbers to the nearest ten, add, and then add or subtract.

$$124 + 268 = ?$$

Think: $120 + 270 = 390$
   $390 + 4 = 394$
   $394 - 2 = 392$

$$124 + 268 = 392$$

Subtraction Facts

10 − 0 = 10	10 − 1 = 9	10 − 2 = 8	10 − 3 = 7
9 − 0 = 9	9 − 1 = 8	9 − 2 = 7	9 − 3 = 6
8 − 0 = 8	8 − 1 = 7	8 − 2 = 6	8 − 3 = 5
7 − 0 = 7	7 − 1 = 6	7 − 2 = 5	7 − 3 = 4
6 − 0 = 6	6 − 1 = 5	6 − 2 = 4	6 − 3 = 3
5 − 0 = 5	5 − 1 = 4	5 − 2 = 3	5 − 3 = 2
4 − 0 = 4	4 − 1 = 3	4 − 2 = 2	4 − 3 = 1
3 − 0 = 3	3 − 1 = 2	3 − 2 = 1	3 − 3 = 0
2 − 0 = 2	2 − 1 = 1	2 − 2 = 0	
1 − 0 = 1	1 − 1 = 0		
0 − 0 = 0			

10 − 4 = 6	10 − 5 = 5	10 − 6 = 4	10 − 7 = 3
9 − 4 = 5	9 − 5 = 4	9 − 6 = 3	9 − 7 = 2
8 − 4 = 4	8 − 5 = 3	8 − 6 = 2	8 − 7 = 1
7 − 4 = 3	7 − 5 = 2	7 − 6 = 1	7 − 7 = 0
6 − 4 = 2	6 − 5 = 1	6 − 6 = 0	
5 − 4 = 1	5 − 5 = 0		
4 − 4 = 0			

10 − 8 = 2	10 − 9 = 1	10 − 10 = 0
9 − 8 = 1	9 − 9 = 0	
8 − 8 = 0		

Subtraction Strategies

Count back.

Count backward from the minuend.

14 – 5 = ?

Think:
14 > 1
13 > 2
12 > 3
11 > 4
10 > 5
9

14 – 5 = 9

Add to check.

Add the difference and the subtrahend to equal the minuend.

18 – 3 = ?

Think: 15 + 3 = 18

18 – 3 = 15

Use related addition facts.

Use the related addition fact to find the difference.

12 – 8 = ?

Think: 8 + 4 = 12

12 – 8 = 4

Build on doubles.

Use the nearest doubles fact.

17 – 8 = ?

Think: 16 – 8 = 8
8 + 1 = 9

17 – 8 = 9

Subtract the places.

Change one number to its expanded form and subtract the larger number first.

46 – 24 = ?

Think: 24 is 20 + 4
46 – 20 = 26
26 – 4 = 22

46 – 24 = 22

Multiplication Facts

0 x 0 = 0	0 x 1 = 0	0 x 2 = 0	0 x 3 = 0	0 x 4 = 0
1 x 0 = 0	1 x 1 = 1	1 x 2 = 2	1 x 3 = 3	1 x 4 = 4
2 x 0 = 0	2 x 1 = 2	2 x 2 = 4	2 x 3 = 6	2 x 4 = 8
3 x 0 = 0	3 x 1 = 3	3 x 2 = 6	3 x 3 = 9	3 x 4 = 12
4 x 0 = 0	4 x 1 = 4	4 x 2 = 8	4 x 3 = 12	4 x 4 = 16
5 x 0 = 0	5 x 1 = 5	5 x 2 = 10	5 x 3 = 15	5 x 4 = 20
6 x 0 = 0	6 x 1 = 6	6 x 2 = 12	6 x 3 = 18	6 x 4 = 24
7 x 0 = 0	7 x 1 = 7	7 x 2 = 14	7 x 3 = 21	7 x 4 = 28
8 x 0 = 0	8 x 1 = 8	8 x 2 = 16	8 x 3 = 24	8 x 4 = 32
9 x 0 = 0	9 x 1 = 9	9 x 2 = 18	9 x 3 = 27	9 x 4 = 36
10 x 0 = 0	10 x 1 = 10	10 x 2 = 20	10 x 3 = 30	10 x 4 = 40
11 x 0 = 0	11 x 1 = 11	11 x 2 = 22	11 x 3 = 33	11 x 4 = 44
12 x 0 = 0	12 x 1 = 12	12 x 2 = 24	12 x 3 = 36	12 x 4 = 48

0 x 5 = 0	0 x 6 = 0	0 x 7 = 0	0 x 8 = 0	0 x 8 = 0
1 x 5 = 5	1 x 6 = 6	1 x 7 = 7	1 x 8 = 8	1 x 9 = 9
2 x 5 = 10	2 x 6 = 12	2 x 7 = 14	2 x 8 = 16	2 x 9 = 18
3 x 5 = 15	3 x 6 = 18	3 x 7 = 21	3 x 8 = 24	3 x 9 = 27
4 x 5 = 20	4 x 6 = 24	4 x 7 = 28	4 x 8 = 32	4 x 9 = 36
5 x 5 = 25	5 x 6 = 30	5 x 7 = 35	5 x 8 = 40	5 x 9 = 45
6 x 5 = 30	6 x 6 = 36	6 x 7 = 42	6 x 8 = 48	6 x 9 = 54
7 x 5 = 35	7 x 6 = 42	7 x 7 = 49	7 x 8 = 56	7 x 9 = 63
8 x 5 = 40	8 x 6 = 48	8 x 7 = 56	8 x 8 = 64	8 x 9 = 72
9 x 5 = 45	9 x 6 = 54	9 x 7 = 63	9 x 8 = 72	9 x 9 = 81
10 x 5 = 50	10 x 6 = 60	10 x 7 = 70	10 x 8 = 80	10 x 9 = 90
11 x 5 = 55	11 x 6 = 66	11 x 7 = 77	11 x 8 = 88	11 x 9 = 99
12 x 5 = 60	12 x 6 = 72	12 x 7 = 84	12 x 8 = 96	12 x 9 = 108

0 x 10 = 0	0 x 11 = 0	0 x 12 = 0
1 x 10 = 10	1 x 11 = 11	1 x 12 = 12
2 x 10 = 20	2 x 11 = 22	2 x 12 = 24
3 x 10 = 30	3 x 11 = 33	3 x 12 = 36
4 x 10 = 40	4 x 11 = 44	4 x 12 = 48
5 x 10 = 50	5 x 11 = 55	5 x 12 = 60
6 x 10 = 60	6 x 11 = 66	6 x 12 = 72
7 x 10 = 70	7 x 11 = 77	7 x 12 = 84
8 x 10 = 80	8 x 11 = 88	8 x 12 = 96
9 x 10 = 90	9 x 11 = 99	9 x 12 = 108
10 x 10 = 100	10 x 11 = 110	10 x 12 = 120
11 x 10 = 110	11 x 11 = 121	11 x 12 = 132
12 x 10 = 120	12 x 11 = 132	12 x 12 = 144

Multiplication Strategies

Repeat addition.

Use addition to solve multiplication.

$$8 \times 4 = ?$$

Think:
$$\begin{array}{r} 8 \\ 8 \\ 8 \\ +\,8 \\ \hline 32 \end{array}$$

$$8 \times 4 = 32$$

Skip count.

Count by a familiar number pattern.

$$6 \times 5 = ?$$

5
10
15
20
25
30

$$6 \times 5 = 30$$

Anchor facts.

Use familiar multiplication facts to solve more difficult ones.

$$11 \times 13 = ?$$

Think: $13 = 10 + 3$
Then $11 \times 10 = 110$
and $11 \times 3 = 33$
$33 + 110 = 143$

$$11 \times 13 = 143$$

Multiply by two.

Double the other factor.

$$7 \times 2 = ?$$

Think: $7 + 7 = 14$

$$7 \times 2 = 14$$

Multiply by three.

Double the other factor and then add one set.

$$8 \times 3 = ?$$

Think: $8 + 8 = 16$
$16 + 8 = 24$

$$8 \times 3 = 24$$

Multiply by four.

Double the other factor and then double the sum.

$$9 \times 4 = ?$$

Think: $9 + 9 = 18$
$18 + 18 = 36$

$$9 \times 4 = 36$$

Multiply by eight.

Double the other factor and then double the sum two more times.

$$6 \times 8 = ?$$

Think: $6 + 6 = 12$
$12 + 12 = 24$
$24 + 24 = 48$

$$6 \times 8 = 48$$

Multiply by nine.

Multiply the other factor by 10 and then subtract it from the product.

$$9 \times 6 = ?$$

Think: $10 \times 6 = 60$
$60 - 6 = 54$

$$9 \times 6 = 54$$

Division Facts

$0 \div 1 = 0$	$0 \div 2 = 0$	$0 \div 3 = 0$	$0 \div 4 = 0$	$0 \div 5 = 0$
$1 \div 1 = 1$	$2 \div 2 = 1$	$3 \div 3 = 1$	$4 \div 4 = 1$	$5 \div 5 = 1$
$2 \div 1 = 2$	$4 \div 2 = 2$	$6 \div 3 = 2$	$8 \div 4 = 2$	$10 \div 5 = 2$
$3 \div 1 = 3$	$6 \div 2 = 3$	$9 \div 3 = 3$	$12 \div 4 = 3$	$15 \div 5 = 3$
$4 \div 1 = 4$	$8 \div 2 = 4$	$12 \div 3 = 4$	$16 \div 4 = 4$	$20 \div 5 = 4$
$5 \div 1 = 5$	$10 \div 2 = 5$	$15 \div 3 = 5$	$20 \div 4 = 5$	$25 \div 5 = 5$
$6 \div 1 = 6$	$12 \div 2 = 6$	$18 \div 3 = 6$	$24 \div 4 = 6$	$30 \div 5 = 6$
$7 \div 1 = 7$	$14 \div 2 = 7$	$21 \div 3 = 7$	$28 \div 4 = 7$	$35 \div 5 = 7$
$8 \div 1 = 8$	$16 \div 2 = 8$	$24 \div 3 = 8$	$32 \div 4 = 8$	$40 \div 5 = 8$
$9 \div 1 = 9$	$18 \div 2 = 9$	$27 \div 3 = 9$	$36 \div 4 = 9$	$45 \div 5 = 9$
$10 \div 1 = 10$	$20 \div 2 = 10$	$30 \div 3 = 10$	$40 \div 4 = 10$	$50 \div 5 = 10$
$11 \div 1 = 11$	$22 \div 2 = 11$	$33 \div 3 = 11$	$44 \div 4 = 11$	$55 \div 5 = 11$
$12 \div 1 = 12$	$24 \div 2 = 12$	$36 \div 3 = 12$	$48 \div 4 = 12$	$60 \div 5 = 12$

$0 \div 6 = 0$	$0 \div 7 = 0$	$0 \div 8 = 0$	$0 \div 9 = 0$	$0 \div 10 = 0$
$6 \div 6 = 1$	$7 \div 7 = 1$	$8 \div 8 = 1$	$9 \div 9 = 1$	$10 \div 10 = 1$
$12 \div 6 = 2$	$14 \div 7 = 2$	$16 \div 8 = 2$	$18 \div 9 = 2$	$20 \div 10 = 2$
$18 \div 6 = 3$	$21 \div 7 = 3$	$24 \div 8 = 3$	$27 \div 9 = 3$	$30 \div 10 = 3$
$24 \div 6 = 4$	$28 \div 7 = 4$	$32 \div 8 = 4$	$36 \div 9 = 4$	$40 \div 10 = 4$
$30 \div 6 = 5$	$35 \div 7 = 5$	$40 \div 8 = 5$	$45 \div 9 = 5$	$50 \div 10 = 5$
$36 \div 6 = 6$	$42 \div 7 = 6$	$48 \div 8 = 6$	$54 \div 9 = 6$	$60 \div 10 = 6$
$42 \div 6 = 7$	$49 \div 7 = 7$	$56 \div 8 = 7$	$63 \div 9 = 7$	$70 \div 10 = 7$
$48 \div 6 = 8$	$56 \div 7 = 8$	$64 \div 8 = 8$	$72 \div 9 = 8$	$80 \div 10 = 8$
$54 \div 6 = 9$	$63 \div 7 = 9$	$72 \div 8 = 9$	$81 \div 9 = 9$	$90 \div 10 = 9$
$60 \div 6 = 10$	$70 \div 7 = 10$	$80 \div 8 = 10$	$90 \div 9 = 10$	$100 \div 10 = 10$
$66 \div 6 = 11$	$77 \div 7 = 11$	$88 \div 8 = 11$	$99 \div 9 = 11$	$110 \div 10 = 11$
$72 \div 6 = 12$	$84 \div 7 = 12$	$96 \div 8 = 12$	$108 \div 9 = 12$	$120 \div 10 = 12$

$0 \div 11 = 0$	$0 \div 12 = 0$
$11 \div 11 = 1$	$12 \div 12 = 1$
$22 \div 11 = 2$	$24 \div 12 = 2$
$33 \div 11 = 3$	$36 \div 12 = 3$
$44 \div 11 = 4$	$48 \div 12 = 4$
$55 \div 11 = 5$	$60 \div 12 = 5$
$66 \div 11 = 6$	$72 \div 12 = 6$
$77 \div 11 = 7$	$84 \div 12 = 7$
$88 \div 11 = 8$	$96 \div 12 = 8$
$99 \div 11 = 9$	$108 \div 12 = 9$
$110 \div 11 = 10$	$120 \div 12 = 10$
$121 \div 11 = 11$	$132 \div 12 = 11$
$132 \div 11 = 12$	$144 \div 12 = 12$

Division Strategies

Repeat subtraction.

20 ÷ 4 = ?

Think:

```
   20
 -  4
   16
 -  4
   12
 -  4
    8
 -  4
    4
 -  4
    0
```

20 ÷ 4 = 5

Draw a picture.

10 ÷ 2 = ?

10 ÷ 2 = 5

Make a model.

12 ÷ 3 = ?

12 ÷ 3 = 4

Use arrays.

15 ÷ 5 = ?

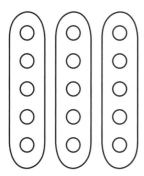

15 ÷ 5 = 3

Use related multiplication facts.

Think: 28 ÷ 7 = ?

7 × ? = 28

7 × 4 = 28,

so

28 ÷ 7 = 4

Use partial quotients.

472 ÷ 6 = ?

```
6)472  | 50
-300   |
 172   | 20
-120   |
  52   | + 8
- 48   |
   4   | 78 R4
```

472 ÷ 6 = 78 R4

Customary Measurements

Length
foot = 12 inches
yard = 3 feet, or 36 inches
mile = 1,760 yards, or 5,280 feet,
    or 63,360 inches

Area
square foot = 144 square inches
square yard = 9 square feet
acre = 4,840 square yards,
    or 43,560 square feet

Weight
pound = 16 ounces
ton = 2,000 pounds, or 32,000 ounces

Volume
cubic foot = 1,728 cubic inches
cubic yard = 27 cubic feet

Capacity
tablespoon = 3 teaspoons
fluid ounce = 2 tablespoons
cup = 8 fluid ounces, or 16 tablespoons
pint = 2 cups, or 16 fluid ounces
quart = 2 pints, or 4 cups, or 32 fluid ounces
half-gallon = 2 quarts, or 4 pints, or 8 cups, or 64 fluid ounces
gallon = 4 quarts, or 8 pints, or 16 cups, or 128 fluid ounces

Time
minute = 60 seconds
hour = 60 minutes
day = 24 hours
week = 7 days
year = $365\frac{1}{4}$ days, or 52 weeks

Temperature
degrees Fahrenheit (°F)

Metric Measurements

Length
centimeter = 10 millimeters
decimeter = 10 centimeters
meter = 10 decimeters, or
100 centimeters
kilometer = 1,000 meters

Mass
centigram = 10 milligrams
gram = 1,000 milligrams
kilogram = 1,000 grams
metric ton = 1,000 kilograms

Capacity
centiliter = 10 milliliters
liter = 1,000 milliliters
kiloliter = 1,000 liters

Area
square centimeter = 100 square
millimeters
square decimeter = 100 square
centimeters
hectare = 10,000 square
meters

Volume
cubic centimeter = 1,000 cubic millimeters
cubic decimeter = 1,000 cubic centimeters
cubic meter = 1,000,000 cubic centimeters

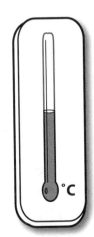

Temperature
degrees Celsius (°C)

Plane Shapes

acute angle
angle
closed figure
compass
congruent figure
intersecting lines
line
line of symmetry
line segment
midpoint
obtuse angle
open figure
parallel lines
perpendicular lines
plane

point
protractor
ray
reflection (flip)
right angle
rotation (turn)
rotational symmetry
side
similar figures
symmetry
tessellation
transformation
translation (slide)
two-dimensional
vertex

polygon
regular polygon
circle
   center
   central angle
   chord
   circumference
   diameter
   radius
triangle
   acute
   obtuse
   right
   equilateral
   isosceles
   scalene

quadrilateral
  trapezoid
  parallelogram
    rectangle
    rhombus
    square
pentagon
hexagon
heptagon
octagon
nonagon
decagon

area
perimeter
length
width

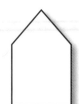

Solid Figures

apex

base

edge

face

net

three-dimensional

vertex

volume

cubic unit

height

length

width

polyhedron

  cube

  hexagonal prism

  pentagonal prism

  rectangular prism

  triangular prism

  rectangular pyramid

  square pyramid

  triangular pyramid

cone

cylinder

sphere

Properties

Rules about numbers that are always true.

✛ ✛ ✛ Properties of Addition ✛ ✛ ✛

Commutative (Order) Property:
Changing the order of two addends does not change the sum.

$$5 + 3 = 8 \qquad 3 + 5 = 8$$

Associative (Grouping) Property:
Changing the grouping of three or more addends does not change the sum.

$$(7 + 3) + 4 = 14 \qquad 7 + (3 + 4) = 14$$

Identity (Zero) Property:
When you add zero to any addend, the sum will always equal the addend.

$$2 + 0 = 2 \qquad 0 + 17 = 17$$

✛ ₋ ÷ ✕ Properties of Equality ✛ ₋ ÷ ✕

Addition: When you add the same addend to both sides of an equation, the products remain equal.

If $6 + 8 = 9 + 5$,
then $6 + 8 + 7 = 9 + 5 + 7$.

Subtraction: When you subtract the same subtrahend from both sides of an equation, the differences remain equal.

If $17 - 9 = 8$,
then $(17 - 9) - 2 = 8 - 2$.

Multiplication: When you multiply both sides of an equation by the same factor, the products remain equal.

If $3 \times 6 = 9 \times 2$,
then $3 \times 6 \times 4 = 9 \times 2 \times 4$.

Division: When you divide both sides of an equation by the same divisor (except for 0), the quotient remains equal.

If $11 + 5 = 16$,
then $(11 + 5) \div 4 = 16 \div 4$.

✕ ✕ ✕ ✕ Properties of Multiplication ✕ ✕ ✕ ✕

Commutative (Order) Property:
Changing the order of two factors does not change the product.

$$7 \times 3 = 21$$
$$3 \times 7 = 21$$

Associative (Grouping) Property:
Changing the grouping of factors does not change the product.

$$(6 \times 5) \times 3 = 90$$
$$6 \times (5 \times 3) = 90$$

Distributive Property:
Separating numbers into parts does not change the product. You can multiply a sum by multiplying each addend by itself and then adding the products.

$$5 \times 62 =$$
$$5 \times (60 + 2) =$$
$$(5 \times 60) + (5 \times 2) =$$
$$300 + 10 = 310$$

The distributive property can be used to make larger numbers easier to multiply.

$$4 \times 197 = 4 (200 - 3)$$
$$= (4 \times 200) - (4 \times 3)$$
$$= 800 - 12$$
$$= 788$$

Identity (Multiplying by One) Property:
When you multiply any factor by one, the product will always equal the factor.

$$12 \times 1 = 12 \qquad 1 \times 9 = 9$$

Zero Property:
When you multiply any factor by zero, the product will always equal zero.

$$7 \times 0 = 0 \qquad 0 \times 11 = 0$$

Formulas

Perimeter

Squares:

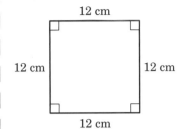

$p = 4 \text{ x side}$
$p = 4 \text{ x } s$
$p = 4 \text{ x } 12 = 48 \text{ cm}$

Rectangles:

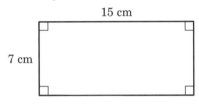

$p = (2 \text{ x length}) + (2 \text{ x width})$
$p = (2 \text{ x } l) + (2 \text{ x } w)$
$p = (2 \text{ x } 15) + (2 \text{ x } 7)$
$p = 30 + 14 = 44 \text{ cm}$

Area

Squares:

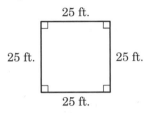

$a = \text{side x side} = s^2$
$a = 25 \text{ ft. x } 25 \text{ ft.}$
$\quad = (25 \text{ ft.})^2$
$a = 625 \text{ sq. ft.}$
$\quad = 625 \text{ ft.}^2$

Rectangles:

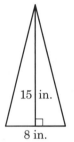

$a = \text{length x width} = l \text{ x } w$
$a = 41 \text{ ft. x } 76 \text{ ft.}$
$a = 3{,}116 \text{ sq. ft.}$
$\quad = 3{,}116 \text{ ft.}^2$

Parallelograms:

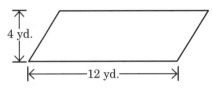

$a = \text{base x height}$
$a = b \text{ x } h$
$a = 4 \text{ yd. x } 12 \text{ yd.} = 48 \text{ yd.}^2$

Triangles:

$a = \tfrac{1}{2} \text{ x base x height}$
$a = \tfrac{1}{2} \text{ x } b \text{ x } h$
$a = \tfrac{1}{2} \text{ x } 8 \text{ in. x } 15 \text{ in.} = 60 \text{ in.}^2$

Circumference

Circles:

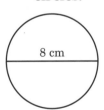

$c = \pi \text{ x } d$
$c = 3.14 \text{ x } 8$
$c = 25.12 \text{ cm}$

Hint: diameter = 2 x radius
$c = \pi \text{ x } 2 \text{ x } r \textbf{ or } c = 2 \text{ x } \pi \text{ x } r$
$c = 2 \text{ x } 3.14 \text{ x } 3$
$c = 18.84 \text{ in.}$

Surface Area

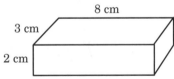

2 x (area of front) + 2 x (area of top) + 2 x (area of left)
$2 \text{ x } (2 \text{ x } 8) + 2 \text{ x } (3 \text{ x } 8) + 2 \text{ x } (2 \text{ x } 3) = 92 \text{ cm}^2$

Volume

Rectangular Prism

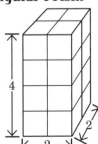

$v = (l \text{ x } w) \text{ x } h \textbf{ or } v = b \text{ x } h$
$v = (l \text{ x } w) \text{ x } h$
$\quad = (2 \text{ x } 2) \text{ x } 4$
$\quad = 16 \text{ units}^3$

Problem-Solving Strategies

❋ Act It Out

❋ Draw a Picture

❋ Guess, Check, and Revise

❋ Look for a Pattern

❋ Make a List

❋ Make a Table

❋ Work Backward

❋ Write a Number Sentence

Clue Words for Story Problems

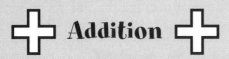

✚ Addition ✚

add	in all
additional	increased by
all	plus
all together	raise
altogether	sum
both	together
combined	total

▭ Subtraction ▭

are not	have left
change (money	how much more
problems)	less than
changed	lost
decreased by	more
difference	reduced
dropped	remain
exceeded	subtract
fewer	take away

comparisons: How much heavier? younger? smaller? more than?

➗ Division ➗

as much	half for a
cut	fraction
cut up	out of
divided	parts
divisor	quotient of
each	separated
equal parts	shared
every	split
find the average	

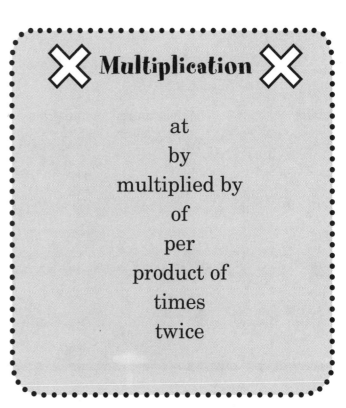

✖ Multiplication ✖

at
by
multiplied by
of
per
product of
times
twice

Math Prefixes and Suffixes

Prefixes

prefix	meaning	example
bi-	two	bisect
cent-, centi-	one hundredth	centiliter
circum-	around	circumference
dec-, deca-, deka-	ten	decade
deci-	one tenth	decimeter
di-	two, twice, double	dimeter
dodeca-	twelve	dodecagon
equi-	equal, equally	equilateral
giga-	billion	gigawatt
hecto-	100	hectoliter
hemi-	half	hemisphere
hepta-	seven	heptagon
hex-, hexa-	six	hexagon
kilo-	1,000	kiloliter
mid-	middle	midpoint
milli-	one thousandth	milligram
nona-	nine	nonagon
oct-, octa-, octo-	eight	octagon
pent-, penta-	five	pentagon
per-	for each	percentage
poly-	many	polyhedron
quad-	four	quadruple
semi-	half	semiannual
tri-	three	triple

Suffixes

suffix	meaning	example
-centenary	refers to a 100-year period	bicentenary
-gon	figures with angles	decagon
-hedron	figures with faces or surfaces	dihedron
-lateral	relating to sides	trilateral
-meter, -metry	measuring	perimeter
-sect	cut or divide	bisect

Roman Numerals

I	= 1	XL	= 40
II	= 2	L	= 50
III	= 3	LX	= 60
IV	= 4	LXX	= 70
V	= 5	LXXX	= 80
VI	= 6	XC	= 90
VII	= 7	C	= 100
VIII	= 8	D	= 500
IX	= 9	M	= 1,000
X	= 10	$\overline{V}$	= 5,000
XX	= 20	$\overline{X}$	= 10,000
XXX	= 30		

Fractions

numerator: top number in a fraction; it tells how many equal parts $\frac{2}{4}$

denominator: bottom number in a fraction; it tells the total number of parts $\frac{2}{4}$

common denominators: a common multiple for the denominators of two or more fractions; also called *like denominators*
12 is a common denominator for $\frac{1}{3}$ and $\frac{1}{4}$

equivalent fractions: fractions with the same value $\frac{1}{2}, \frac{2}{4}, \frac{3}{6}$

improper fraction: a fraction with a value greater than one but not written as a mixed number $\frac{6}{3}$

least common denominator (LCD): the least common multiple for the denominator of two or more fractions
15 is the LCD for $\frac{2}{3}$ and $\frac{1}{5}$

like fractions: fractions with the same denominator $\frac{3}{8}$ and $\frac{5}{8}$

mixed number: a number that includes a whole number (not zero) and a fraction $3\frac{1}{3}$

simplest form: a fraction whose numerator and denominator's only common factor is one

like denominators (common denominators): also called lowest terms $\frac{2}{8}$ $\frac{1}{4}$

unit fraction: a fraction that has one as its numerator $\frac{1}{2}, \frac{1}{3}, \frac{1}{4}, \frac{1}{5}$

Fraction and Decimal Equivalents

$\frac{1}{100} = 0.01$	$\frac{2}{10} = 0.2$	$\frac{1}{2} = 0.5$	$\frac{5}{6} = 0.833...$
$\frac{2}{100} = 0.02$	$\frac{25}{100} = 0.25$	$\frac{1}{3} = 0.333...$	$\frac{1}{8} = 0.125$
$\frac{3}{100} = 0.03$	$\frac{3}{10} = 0.3$	$\frac{2}{3} = 0.666...$	$\frac{3}{8} = 0.375$
$\frac{4}{100} = 0.04$	$\frac{4}{10} = 0.4$	$\frac{1}{4} = 0.25$	$\frac{5}{8} = 0.625$
$\frac{5}{100} = 0.05$	$\frac{5}{10}$ and $\frac{50}{100} = 0.5$	$\frac{2}{4} = 0.5$	$\frac{7}{8} = 0.875$
$\frac{6}{100} = 0.06$	$\frac{6}{10} = 0.6$	$\frac{3}{4} = 0.75$	$\frac{1}{9} = 0.111...$
$\frac{7}{100} = 0.07$	$\frac{7}{10} = 0.7$	$\frac{1}{5} = 0.2$	$\frac{2}{9} = 0.222...$
$\frac{8}{100} = 0.08$	$\frac{75}{100} = 0.75$	$\frac{2}{5} = 0.4$	$\frac{4}{9} = 0.444...$
$\frac{9}{100} = 0.09$	$\frac{8}{10} = 0.8$	$\frac{3}{5} = 0.6$	$\frac{5}{9} = 0.555...$
$\frac{1}{10}$ and $\frac{10}{100} = 0.1$	$\frac{9}{10} = 0.9$	$\frac{4}{5} = 0.8$	$\frac{7}{9} = 0.777...$
	$\frac{10}{10} = 1.0$	$\frac{1}{6} = 0.166...$	$\frac{8}{9} = 0.888...$

Data and Graphing
Ways to Display Data

Bar Graphs	Line Plots	Tables
Circle Graphs	Picture Graphs	Tally Charts
Line Graphs	Stem-and-Leaf Plots	Venn Diagrams

Terms

average: a number found by dividing the sum of a set of numbers by the number of addends

axis: lines at the side or bottom of a graph; the *x*-axis (*abscissa*) is the horizontal axis. The *y*-axis (*ordinate*) is the vertical axis.

axes: the plural form of *axis*

bar graph: a graph that uses bars to represent countable data

circle graph: a graph that shows information as parts of a circle, in percentages; also called a *pie graph*

frequency: the number of times an event or action occurs during a set time period

graph: a picture that displays gathered facts in an organized way; a complete graph includes a title, subtitle, labeled axes, and a key (when needed)

interval: the amount of time or space between two items or incidents; the group of numbers between two set numbers or points

line graph: a graph that uses lines to show change over time

line plot: a graph that shows the frequency of data along a number line

mean: the average of a set of numbers

median: the middle number in a set of sequentially ordered numbers

mode: the number that occurs most often in a set of numbers

picture graph: a graph that uses pictures to symbolize information; also called a *pictograph*

range: the difference between the greatest and least number in a set of numbers

sample: an example; a small part of something used to represent the whole group; can be used to make inferences about the rest of the group

statistics: numerical facts that can be put into a table to show information about a specific topic

stem-and-leaf plot: groups of data displayed by place value

survey: a method of gathering information or opinions from a group of people

tally marks: lines on a tally chart; used to keep track of information

Venn diagram: a diagram of overlapping circles that shows the relationship between or among sets of data

Graph Topics

Do you like to wear gloves or mittens?

Have you ever been hiking?

Have you ever been on an airplane?

How many letters are in your name?

How many pencils are in your desk?

How many people are in your family?

How many pockets are on your clothing?

How many states have you visited?

How many teeth have you lost?

In which month were you born?

What kind of pet do you have?

What time did you wake this morning?

What's the first letter in your name?

What's your favorite thing to do during recess?

When it rains, do you like to play indoors or outdoors?

Which meal is your favorite?

Which sport do you like to play?

Which type of fruit is your favorite?

Which type of weather do you like the most?

Which word best describes your mood today?

Which zoo animal do you like most?

Would you rather write with a pen or a pencil?

100th Day of School: Items to Group

100-piece puzzle

alphabet blocks

animal-shaped crackers

beans

buttons

cereal

checkers

clothespins

cotton balls

coins

crayons

dice

dominoes

empty spools

game markers

marbles

packing peanuts

pattern blocks

pencils

Ping-Pong balls

plastic bottle caps

plastic eggs

pom-poms

pretzels

seashells

shaped pasta

small cookies

small erasers

stickers or sticky dots

straws

teddy bear counters

Unifix cubes

wrapped candies

Monthly Celebrations

August

- National Inventors' Month
- National Aviation Week (annually, the week that includes August 19)
- 15 National Relaxation Day
- 26 National Dog Day

September

- Labor Day (first Monday)
- 11 Patriot Day
- 17 Constitution Day and Citizenship Day

October

- National Dental Hygiene Month
- 31 Halloween

November

- 11 Veterans Day
- Thanksgiving Day (fourth Thursday)

December

- 7 Pearl Harbor Day
- Hanukkah (starts on the 25th day of Kislev according to the Hebrew calendar)
- 25 Christmas
- 26 Kwanzaa starts (ends January 1)
- 31 New Year's Eve

January

- 1 New Year's Day
- Martin Luther King Day (third Monday)

February

- American Heart Month
- National Black History Month
- National Children's Dental Health Month
- 2 Groundhog Day
- 14 Valentine's Day
- 21 Presidents' Day
- 29 Leap Year Day

March

- Music in Our Schools Month
- Women's History Month
- 2 Dr. Seuss's Birthday Anniversary
- 17 St. Patrick's Day

April

- 1 April Fools' Day
- 14 National D.A.R.E. Day
- 22 Earth Day

May

- 1 May Day
- 5 Cinco de Mayo (Mexico)
- Mother's Day (second Sunday)
- Memorial Day (last Monday)

June

- 14 Flag Day
- Father's Day (third Sunday)

July

- 1 Canada Day (Canada)
- 4 Independence Day

Community Helpers

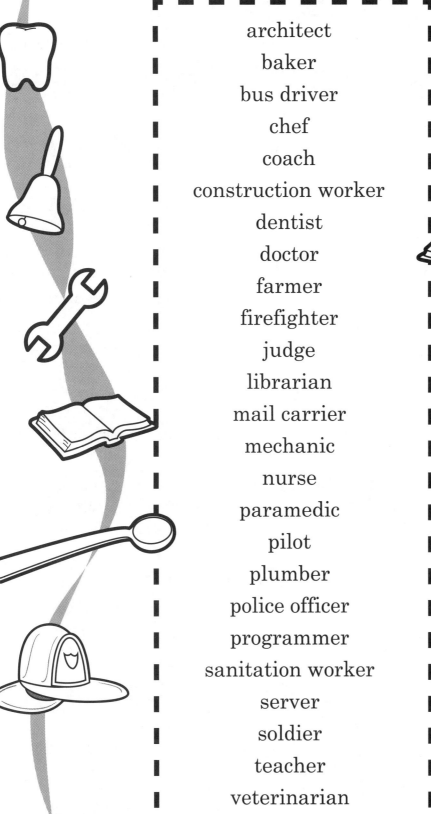
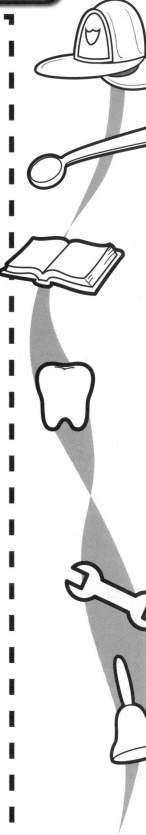

architect
baker
bus driver
chef
coach
construction worker
dentist
doctor
farmer
firefighter
judge
librarian
mail carrier
mechanic
nurse
paramedic
pilot
plumber
police officer
programmer
sanitation worker
server
soldier
teacher
veterinarian

Landforms

archipelago: a stretch of water containing islands

bay: a small body of salt water that reaches into the land; usually smaller than a gulf

canal: a man-made waterway connecting two bodies of water; designed to shorten travel time

canyon: a deep valley with steep sides

channel: a narrow, deep waterway connecting two larger bodies of water

continent: one of the seven largest bodies of land on the earth

delta: land built up by deposits of sand and silt at the mouth of some rivers

desert: a barren region of the earth's surface that receives little rainfall

gulf: part of a sea or ocean that reaches into land; usually larger than a bay

hill: an elevation of the ground that has a distinct summit; smaller in area and height than a mountain

island: a body of land smaller than a continent and surrounded by water

isthmus: a narrow strip of land that connects larger bodies of land

lake: a large body of water surrounded by land

mesa: an isolated hill or mountain that has a flat top and steep sides; usually found in dry climates

mountain: a landform that stands much higher than the surrounding terrain; generally larger than hills; typically has steep slopes and sharp or slightly rounded peaks or ridges

ocean: largest body of salt water

peninsula: an area of land surrounded on three sides by water

plain: a broad, nearly level stretch of land with no sudden changes in elevation

plateau: a raised area of relatively flat land

prairie: a region of flat or hilly land covered chiefly by tall grasses

river: a large stream of water flowing through the land into another body of water

savanna: a grassland with widely scattered trees and shrubs

sea: a large body of water, usually salt water, partly or completely surrounded by land

valley: a natural low point in the earth's surface

volcano: a place where ash, gases, and molten rock from deep underground erupt onto the surface

United States Mountain Ranges and Rivers

Mountain Ranges

Alaskan Range
Appalachian Mountains
Brooks Range
Cascade Range
Coast Ranges

Rocky Mountains (Northern)
Rocky Mountains (Middle)
Rocky Mountains (Southern)
Sierra Nevada

Longest Rivers
(longest to shortest)

1. Missouri
2. Mississippi
3. Yukon
4. Rio Grande
5. St. Lawrence
6. Arkansas
7. Colorado
8. Atchafalaya
9. Ohio
10. Red
11. Brazos
12. Columbia
13. Snake
14. Platte
15. Pecos
16. Canadian
17. Tennessee
18. Colorado (of Texas)
19. North Canadian
20. Mobile
21. Kansas
22. Kuskokwim
23. Yellowstone
24. Tanana
25. Milk
26. Quachita
27. Hamilton
28. Cimarron

Continents and Oceans

Continents
(largest to smallest)

Asia

Africa

North America

South America

Antarctica

Europe

Australia

Oceans
(largest to smallest)

Pacific Ocean

Atlantic Ocean

Indian Ocean

Southern Ocean

Arctic Ocean

Types

general reference maps
    topographic map
    plats
    political map

inventory map

navigation maps
    road map
    street map
    in-vehicle navigation system
    transit map
    aeronautical chart
    nautical chart

thematic map

Terms

atlas
cartographer
cartography
compass rose
degrees
distortion
east
equator
latitude
longitude
map index
map legend
meridians
north
northeast
northern hemisphere
northwest
parallels
prime meridian
scale
south
southeast
southern hemisphere
southwest
west

United States of America

United States Regions

New England States
Connecticut
Maine
Massachusetts
New Hampshire
Rhode Island
Vermont

Midwestern States
Illinois
Indiana
Iowa
Kansas
Michigan
Minnesota
Missouri
Nebraska
North Dakota
Ohio
South Dakota
Wisconsin

Mid-Atlantic States
Delaware
Maryland
New Jersey
New York
Pennsylvania

Rocky Mountain States
Colorado
Idaho
Montana
Nevada
Utah
Wyoming

Southern States
Alabama
Arkansas
Florida
Georgia
Kentucky
Louisiana
Mississippi
North Carolina
South Carolina
Tennessee
Virginia
West Virginia

Southwestern States
Arizona
New Mexico
Oklahoma
Texas

Pacific Coast States
Alaska
California
Hawaii
Oregon
Washington

There are various ways of looking at US regions. Some states can be considered to be in different regions.

US Capitals and States

Montgomery, Alabama	AL		Helena, Montana	MT
Juneau, Alaska	AK		Lincoln, Nebraska	NE
Phoenix, Arizona	AZ		Carson City, Nevada	NV
Little Rock, Arkansas	AR		Concord, New Hampshire	NH
Sacramento, California	CA		Trenton, New Jersey	NJ
Denver, Colorado	CO		Santa Fe, New Mexico	NM
Hartford, Connecticut	CT		Albany, New York	NY
Dover, Delaware	DE		Raleigh, North Carolina	NC
Tallahassee, Florida	FL		Bismarck, North Dakota	ND
Atlanta, Georgia	GA		Columbus, Ohio	OH
Honolulu, Hawaii	HI		Oklahoma City, Oklahoma	OK
Boise, Idaho	ID		Salem, Oregon	OR
Springfield, Illinois	IL		Harrisburg, Pennsylvania	PA
Indianapolis, Indiana	IN		Providence, Rhode Island	RI
Des Moines, Iowa	IA		Columbia, South Carolina	SC
Topeka, Kansas	KS		Pierre, South Dakota	SD
Frankfort, Kentucky	KY		Nashville, Tennessee	TN
Baton Rouge, Louisiana	LA		Austin, Texas	TX
Augusta, Maine	ME		Salt Lake City, Utah	UT
Annapolis, Maryland	MD		Montpelier, Vermont	VT
Boston, Massachusetts	MA		Richmond, Virginia	VA
Lansing, Michigan	MI		Olympia, Washington	WA
St. Paul, Minnesota	MN		Charleston, West Virginia	WV
Jackson, Mississippi	MS		Madison, Wisconsin	WI
Jefferson City, Missouri	MO		Cheyenne, Wyoming	WY

Natural Resources

Alabama—thick pine forests, areas of fertile soil, valuable mineral deposits, deep rivers

Alaska—rich soils, valuable minerals, plentiful water, fish, forests

Arizona—warm climate, mineral deposits

Arkansas—fertile soils, rich mineral deposits, thick forests, abundant water

California—minerals, timber, soil, climate

Colorado—mineral deposits, rich soils, water

Connecticut—forests

Delaware—fertile soil, mineral deposits

Florida—sandy beaches, sunny climate, thick forests, phosphate sand, mineral deposits

Georgia—various mined products, abundant forests, plentiful water supply

Hawaii—plant growth, deep deposits of topsoil, large reservoirs of water

Idaho—fertile soils, vast mineral deposits, plentiful water, dense forests

Illinois—fertile soil, valuable mineral deposits (including coal and petroleum)

Indiana—fertile soil, mineral deposits, plentiful water supply

Iowa—extremely fertile soil, abundant supply of water

Kansas—fertile soil, rich mineral deposits

Kentucky—rich soils, large coal deposits

Louisiana—fertile soils, plentiful deposits of oil and gas, thick forests

Maine—forests, fertile soil, mineral deposits

Maryland—fertile soils, building materials, clays, coal, limestone, natural gas

Massachusetts—fertile river valley soils; deposits of sand, gravel, and other building materials

Michigan—fertile soils, rich mineral deposits, widespread forests, plentiful water, abundant plant and animal life

Minnesota—fertile soil, important minerals, thick evergreen forests

Mississippi—rich soils, abundant water, valuable minerals, large forests

Missouri—fertile soils, large mineral deposits

Natural Resources

Montana—reserves of minerals, cropland, grassland, forestland

Nebraska—soil, water

Nevada—vast mineral deposits, wildlife

New Hampshire—dense forests, minerals

New Jersey—fertile soils, small deposits of minerals

New Mexico—large mineral deposits, forests, grasses, plants, animals

New York—fertile soils, variety of minerals, abundant supplies of water

North Carolina—rich soils, mineral deposits, thick forests

North Dakota—fertile soil, enormous mineral deposits

Ohio—fertile soils, valuable minerals

Oklahoma—vast reserves of minerals, large areas of fertile soil, large supplies of water

Oregon—forestlands, small deposits of many minerals, plentiful water supply, fertile soils

Pennsylvania—rich soils, great mineral wealth, good water supplies, plentiful timber

Rhode Island—a few large mineral deposits

South Carolina—rich soils, minerals, vast forests, plentiful water supply

South Dakota—fertile soil, rich mineral resources

Tennessee—fertile soil, temperate climate, vast water supply, abundant minerals

Texas—large mineral deposits (especially natural gas and petroleum), fertile soils, rich grasslands

Utah—rich mineral deposits, mountain and valley soils

Vermont—mineral deposits, forests, fertile soil

Virginia—varied soils, mineral deposits

Washington—plentiful water supply, large timber reserves, fertile soils

West Virginia—mineral deposits, timber, abundant rainfall

Wisconsin—rich soil, plentiful water, minerals, vast forests

Wyoming—mineral deposits, grazing land, wildlife, water

Social Studies

National Parks

Park	State
Acadia National Park	Maine
Arches National Park	Utah
Badlands National Park	South Dakota
Big Bend National Park	Texas
Biscayne National Park	Florida
Carlsbad Caverns National Park	New Mexico
Channel Islands National Park	California
Crater Lake National Park	Oregon
Cuyahoga Valley National Park	Ohio
Death Valley National Park	California
Everglades National Park	Florida
Glacier National Park	Montana
Grand Canyon National Park	Arizona
Grand Teton National Park	Wyoming
Great Basin National Park	Nevada
Great Smoky Mountains National Park	North Carolina, Tennessee
Hawaii Volcanoes National Park	Hawaii
Hot Springs National Park	Arkansas
Joshua Tree National Park	California
Kenai Fjords National Park	Alaska
Kings Canyon National Park	California
Lassen Volcanic National Park	California
Mammoth Cave National Park	Kentucky
Mesa Verde National Park	Colorado
Mount Rainier National Park	Washington
Redwood National Park	California
Saguaro National Park	Arizona
Sequoia National Park	California
Shenandoah National Park	Virginia
Voyageurs National Park	Minnesota
Wind Cave National Park	South Dakota
Yosemite National Park	California

The Ultimate Teacher's Book of Lists • ©The Mailbox® Books • TEC61339

United States Symbols

Old Glory (flag)

Bald Eagle

Great Seal

Liberty Bell

Rose (national flower)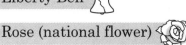

Statue of Liberty

Uncle Sam

United States Capitol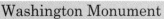

Washington Monument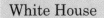

White House

United States Presidents

Name	Term	Name	Term
1. George Washington	1789–1797	23. Benjamin Harrison	1889–1893
2. John Adams	1797–1801	24. Grover Cleveland	1893–1897
3. Thomas Jefferson	1801–1809	25. William McKinley	1897–1901
4. James Monroe	1809–1817	26. Theodore Roosevelt	1901–1909
5. James Madison	1817–1825	27. William Howard Taft	1909–1913
6. John Quincy Adams	1825–1829	28. Woodrow Wilson	1913–1921
7. Andrew Jackson	1829–1837	29. Warren G. Harding	1921–1923
8. Martin Van Buren	1837–1841	30. Calvin Coolidge	1923–1929
9. William Henry Harrison	1841	31. Herbert Hoover	1929–1933
10. John Tyler	1841–1845	32. Franklin D. Roosevelt	1933–1945
11. James K. Polk	1845–1849	33. Harry S. Truman	1945–1953
12. Zachary Taylor	1849–1850	34. Dwight D. Eisenhower	1953–1961
13. Millard Fillmore	1850–1853	35. John F. Kennedy	1961–1963
14. Franklin Pierce	1853–1857	36. Lyndon B. Johnson	1963–1969
15. James Buchanan	1857–1861	37. Richard M. Nixon	1969–1974
16. Abraham Lincoln	1861–1865	38. Gerald R. Ford	1974–1977
17. Andrew Johnson	1865–1869	39. James "Jimmy" Carter	1977–1981
18. Ulysses S. Grant	1869–1877	40. Ronald Reagan	1981–1989
19. Rutherford B. Hayes	1877–1881	41. George H. W. Bush	1989–1993
20. James Garfield	1881	42. William "Bill" Clinton	1993–2001
21. Chester A. Arthur	1881–1885	43. George W. Bush	2001–2009
22. Grover Cleveland	1885–1889	44. Barack Obama	2009–

Social Studies

Influential American Men

William Penn
1644–1718
Founded the Pennsylvania colony

Benjamin Franklin
1706–90
Ran a colonial newspaper; wrote *Poor Richard's Almanack*; served on the Continental Congress during the American Revolution; helped draft both the Declaration of Independence and the Constitution

George Washington
1732–99
Is called the Father of His Country; commanded the army during the American Revolution and became the country's first president

John Adams
1735–1826
Lead thinker in the American Revolution; served on the Continental Congress; helped draft the Declaration of Independence; first American vice president; second American president

Patrick Henry
1736–99
Great orator and leader in the American Revolution; spoke the famous line "Give me liberty or give me death!"

Thomas Paine
1737–1809
Political writer; penned *Common Sense*, the first pamphlet calling for American independence and democratic government

Thomas Jefferson
1743–1826
Wrote the Declaration of Independence; third president of the United States

James Madison
1751–1836
Fourth president of the United States; authored the Bill of Rights for the Constitution

Henry Clay
1777–1852
Known as the Great Compromiser; promoted peace between the North and South, particularly over the issue of slavery; worked to pass legislation that ultimately helped delay the Civil War for a decade

Robert E. Lee
1807–70
Commander of the Confederate forces during the Civil War

Jefferson Davis
1808–89
President of the Confederate States of America during the Civil War

Abraham Lincoln
1809–65
Sixteenth president of the United States; known as the Great Emancipator; signed the Emancipation Proclamation in 1863

Frederick Douglass
1818–95
Former slave; powerful speaker and writer; argued against slavery and racism; served as advisor to President Lincoln

Mark Twain (Samuel Clemens)
1835–1910
Authored *The Adventures of Huckleberry Finn*; writings were influential in developing the course of American literature

John D. Rockefeller
1839–1937
Industrialist in the American petroleum industry; became well-known for his philanthropic generosity

Thomas Edison
1847–1931
Invented such things as the phonograph (sound) recording and electric lighting

Henry Ford
1863–1947
Developed and implemented ideas for manufacturing inexpensive automobiles, most notably the assembly-line principle

Cesar Chavez
1927–93
Started a farm workers' union and devoted his life to improving conditions for America's poorest workers

Martin Luther King Jr.
1929–68
Articulate, charismatic speaker for and leader of the civil rights movement; promoted nonviolent protests; was awarded the Nobel Peace Prize in 1964

Ralph Nader
1934–
Activist promoting consumer safety and rights and environmental protection

Colin Powell
1937–
Military hero; first black American appointed as national security advisor and first to serve as chairman of the Joint Chiefs of Staff

Bill Gates
1955–
Computer programmer and software manufacturer; developed operating systems for personal computers; known for his charitable contributions

Influential African Americans

Crispus Attucks
ca. 1723–70
First individual killed in the Boston Massacre; name became a symbol of American resistance during the revolution

Benjamin Banneker
1731–1806
Astronomer, farmer, mathematician, surveyor

Phillis Wheatley
ca. 1753–84
Published a book of poems; first important African American poet

Sojourner Truth
ca. 1797–1883
Spoke in support of African Americans' freedom and welfare as well as women's rights

Dred Scott
ca. 1799–1858
Filed a lawsuit for his freedom after his master moved him from a slave state to a free one; the Supreme Court ruled that he was not free, sparking controversy between proslavery and antislavery parties.

Nat Turner
ca. 1800–31
Led a one-day rebellion in which black slaves went from farm to farm killing white people; although unsuccessful, the rebellion did bring attention to the practice of slavery.

Frederick Douglass
1818–95
Former slave who gained fame as a great and powerful speaker and writer; argued against slavery and racism; served as advisor to President Lincoln

Harriet Tubman
ca. 1820–1913
Nurse and spy in the Civil War; best known as the "conductor" of the Underground Railroad, aiding nearly 800 slaves to freedom

Booker T. Washington
1856–1915
Educator who founded the Tuskegee Institute; promoted the economic independence of African Americans

George Washington Carver
ca. 1864–1943
Scientist and educator; revolutionized American agriculture with his theories on crop rotation and soil conservation; created commercial products made from pecans, sweet potatoes, and peanuts

Matthew Henson
1866–1955
Explored the Arctic along with Robert E. Peary; in 1909, he and Peary discovered the North Pole.

Thurgood Marshall
1908–93
First African American appointed as Supreme Court justice

Rosa Parks
1913–2005
Inspired a movement for equality for black Americans after refusing to give up her bus seat to a white man

Shirley Chisholm
1924–2005
First African American woman to serve in the US Congress

Malcolm X (Malcolm Little)
1925–65
Led a civil rights movement promoting African Americans' self-respect and militant defiance

Coretta Scott King
1927–2006
Wife of Martin Luther King Jr.; supported American civil rights; annual book award named in her honor recognizes black American authors and illustrators

Martin Luther King Jr.
1929–68
Articulate, charismatic speaker for and leader of the civil rights movement; promoted nonviolent protests; was awarded the Nobel Peace Prize in 1964

Colin Powell
1937–
Military hero; first black American appointed as national security advisor and first to serve as chairman of the Joint Chiefs of Staff

Frederic D. Gregory
1941–
First African American to command a spaceship

Jesse Jackson
1941–
Civil rights leader, politician, and clergyman

Condoleezza Rice
1954–
First woman to serve as the presidents' national security advisor; first African American woman to become US secretary of state

Barack Obama
1961–
First black American US president (2008); presented with the Nobel Peace Prize in 2009

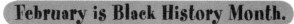

February is Black History Month.

Influential American Women

Abigail Adams
1744–1818
Wife of US President John Adams and mother of US President John Quincy Adams; early supporter of women's rights

Phillis Wheatley
ca. 1753–84
Published a book of poems; first important African American poet

Sacagawea
ca. 1787–1812
Accompanied the Lewis and Clark expedition from 1805 to 1806; Lewis and Clark said they would probably have failed to complete their mission without her help.

Lucretia Mott
1793–1880
Quaker minister, abolitionist, and women's rights activist; formed two antislavery groups; helped organize the first national women's rights meeting

Sojourner Truth
ca. 1797–1883
Spoke in support of African Americans' freedom and welfare as well as women's rights

Harriet Beecher Stowe
1811–96
Wrote the antislavery novel *Uncle Tom's Cabin*

Elizabeth Cady Stanton
1815–1902
Early leader of the women's rights movement; authored the Declaration of the Rights of Women; helped organize the first women's rights convention in the United States

Susan B. Anthony
1820–1906
Helped organize the women's suffrage movement; first woman to be pictured on a US coin in general circulation

Harriet Tubman
ca. 1820–1913
Nurse and spy in the Civil War; best known as the "conductor" of the Underground Railroad, aiding nearly 800 slaves to freedom

Clara Barton
1821–1912
Called the Angel of the Battlefield; gave aid to injured soldiers in the Civil War; founded the American Red Cross

Jane Addams
1860–1935
Social worker, peace activist, and leader for women's suffrage; shared the 1931 Nobel Peace Prize for her work with the Women's International League for Peace and Freedom

Helen Keller
1880–1968
Inspired others with her determination to overcome her blindness and deafness; wrote books, appeared before legislatures, gave lectures, and raised funds to support people with disabilities

Eleanor Roosevelt
1884–1962
One of the most active first ladies in US history; known for her humanitarian efforts for women and minorities

Amelia Earhart
1897–1937
Aviator; promoted the advancement of commercial aviation and the advancement of women

Margaret Mead
1901–78
Anthropologist; found that culture rather than biology determines human behavior; challenged popular beliefs about gender roles, marriage, and cultural values

Grace Hopper
1906–92
American computer scientist; developed a system of translating language into instructions computers could understand

Rachel Carson
1907–64
Writer, environmentalist, and biologist; her warnings about pesticides contaminating the food supply helped launch the environmental movement in the United States

Rosa Parks
1913–2005
Inspired a movement for equality for black Americans after refusing to give up her bus seat to a white man

Shirley Chisholm
1924–2005
First African American woman to serve in the US Congress

Coretta Scott King
1927–2006
Wife of Martin Luther King Jr.; supported American civil rights; annual book award named in her honor recognizes black American authors and illustrators

Sandra Day O'Connor
1930–
First woman to serve on the US Supreme Court

Geraldine Ferraro
1935–2011
First female vice presidential candidate for a major political party

Madeleine Albright
1937–
First female US secretary of state

Hillary Rodham Clinton
1947–
Former US first lady, elected to public office; first woman elected to represent New York in the US Senate; appointed US secretary of state in 2008

Sally Ride
1951–
First American woman to travel in outer space; part of the *Challenger* crew

Condoleezza Rice
1954–
First woman to serve as the presidents' national security advisor; first African American woman to become US secretary of state

Oprah Winfrey
1954–
Producer and host of a television talk show; created an organization that awards hundreds of grants to support women, children, and families

Mae Jemison
1956–
First African American woman to travel in space

Ellen Ochoa
1958–
First Hispanic woman to travel in space

March is National Women's History Month.

Explorers

Marco Polo
ca. 1254–1324
One of the first Europeans to journey into Mongolia and China

John Cabot (Giovanni Caboto)
1450–99
Intended to sail west to reach Asia but explored Newfoundland instead, laying the ground for the British to later claim Canada

Christopher Columbus
1451–1506
In 1492, he set out to find a shortcut from Spain to Asia. Instead, he and his party landed on the Bahamas and claimed it for Spain.

Amerigo Vespucci
ca. 1451–1512
America is named for Vespucci, who said he explored the mainland in 1497.

Vasco da Gama
ca 1460–1524
Sailed from Europe to India by way of the Cape of Good Hope; opened the first all-water trade route between Europe and Asia

Juan Ponce de León
1460–1521
Explored and settled Puerto Rico; also discovered Florida

Vasco Núñez de Balboa
1475–1519
First European to see the Pacific Ocean; claimed the Pacific shores for Spain

Ferdinand Magellan
ca. 1480–1521
Sailed around South America and across the Pacific Ocean; discovered the Strait of Magellan

Hernán Cortés
1485–1547
Known for his march across Mexico; conquered the Aztec Empire

Álvar Núñez Cabeza de Vaca
1490–1560
Explored the Gulf region of present-day Texas

Jacques Cartier
1491–1557
Explored the Canadian coast and the St. Lawrence River; laid the ground for later French claims to parts of North America

Estevanico (Esteban)
ca. 1500–39
Early explorer of the southwestern United States; his tales of treasure inspired Francisco Vásquez de Coronado's explorations

Hernando de Soto
ca. 1500–42
Led the first European expedition to reach the Mississippi River; helped defeat the Incan empire

Francisco Vásquez de Coronado
1510–54
Led an expedition to what is now the American West but never found the treasure he sought

Sir Walter Raleigh
ca. 1552–1618
Sent expedition teams to America; tried to establish an English colony in what is now North Carolina

Henry Hudson
ca. 1565–1611
Attempted to discover a shortcut from Europe to Asia through the Arctic Ocean; a river, strait, and bay in North America bear his name.

Samuel de Champlain
1567–1635
Founded the city of Quebec; combined the French colonies in the New World; discovered Lake Champlain in 1609; explored areas of New York, the Ottawa River, and the eastern Great Lakes

John Smith
1580–1631
Helped establish the first English colony in America

Sieur de La Salle (René-Robert Cavelier)
1643–87
Led the first European expedition to track the Mississippi River to the Gulf of Mexico

Louis Jolliet
ca. 1645–1700
Along with Father Jacques Marquette, he was the first white man to navigate the Mississippi River from the Wisconsin River to the mouth of the Arkansas River.

Jean-Baptiste Le Moyne (Sieur de Bienville)
ca. 1680–1768
Took part in the European settlement of Louisiana and founded New Orleans

William Clark
1770–1838
Along with Meriwether Lewis, led a team in 1803 to explore the Louisiana Purchase

Meriwether Lewis
1774–1809
Along with William Clark, led a team in 1803 to explore the Louisiana Purchase

Zebulon Pike
1779–1813
Explored the Mississippi River in 1805; discovered Pikes Peak, a mountain in Colorado

John Muir
1838–1914
Explored parts of the United States, Europe, Asia, Africa, and the Arctic; fought for the conservation of land, water, and forests in the United States

Robert E. Peary
1856–1920
Explored the Arctic along with Matthew Henson; in 1909, he and Henson discovered the North Pole.

Indians of Early North America

Arctic Indians
Aleut
Inuit
Inupiat
Yupik

Subarctic Indians
Athabaskan
Chipewyan
Cree
Han
Kaska
Naskapi

Indians of the Northwest Coast
Bella Coola
Haida
Makah Chinook
Nootka
Tlingit

Indians of the Plateau
Kakima
Koopena
Nez Perce

California Indians
Chumash
Pomo
Yokuts

Indians of the Great Basin
Paiute
Shoshone
Ute

Indians of the Southwest
Acoma
Apache
Coahuiltec
Hopi
Huichol
Navajo
Pueblo
Toho'no-o-otam
Yaqui
Zuni

Indians of the Plains
Arapaho
Assiniboine
Blackfoot
Cheyenne
Comanche
Cree
Crow
Iowa
Kaw
Kiowa
Mandan
Missouri
Omaha
Osage
Pawnee
Quapaw
Sioux

Indians of Middle America
Aztec
Maya
Mixtec
Toltec
Zapotec

Indians of the Caribbean
Mosquito

Indians of the Eastern Woodlands
Algonkin
Beothuk
Caddo
Calusa
Cherokee
Chickasaw
Chippewa (Ojibwa)
Choctaw
Delaware
Erie
Huron
Illinois
Iroquois
Iroquois League
    Cayuga
    Mohawk
    Oneida
    Onondaga
    Seneca
Massuchuset
Miami
Micmac
Natchez
Ottawa
Penobscot
Powhatan
Sauk Fox
Shawnee
Timucua
Tuscarora
Yuchi

Who Signed the US Constitution?

Thirty-nine delegates signed the Constitution on September 17, 1787.

Connecticut
William Samuel Johnson
Roger Sherman

Delaware
Richard Bassett
Gunning Bedford Jr.
Jacob Broom
John Dickinson
George Read

Georgia
Abraham Baldwin
William Few

Maryland
Daniel Carroll
Daniel of St. Thomas Jenifer
James McHenry

Massachusetts
Nathaniel Gorham
Rufus King

New Hampshire
Nicholas Gilman
John Langdon

New Jersey
David Brearley
Jonathan Dayton
William Livingston
William Paterson

New York
Alexander Hamilton

North Carolina
William Blount
Richard Dobbs Spaight
Hugh Williamson

Pennsylvania
George Clymer
Thomas FitzSimons
Benjamin Franklin
Jared Ingersoll
Thomas Mifflin
Gouverneur Morris
Robert Morris
James Wilson

South Carolina
Pierce Butler
Charles Cotesworth Pinckney
Charles Pinckney
John Rutledge

Virginia
John Blair
James Madison Jr.
George Washington

Branches of United States Government

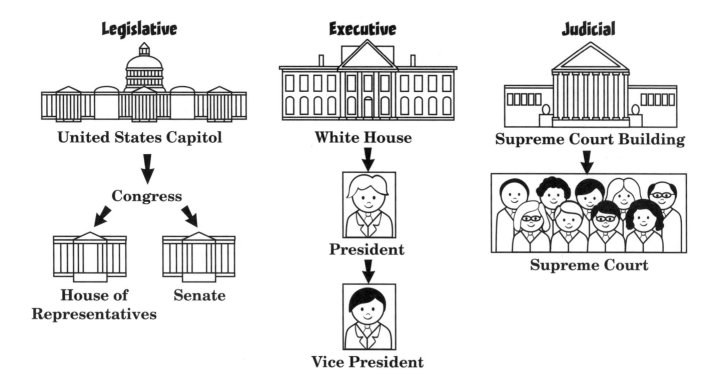

Legislative

United States Capitol

↓

Congress

↙ ↘

House of Representatives   Senate

Executive

White House

↓

President

↓

Vice President

Judicial

Supreme Court Building

↓

Supreme Court

Legislative Branch of Government
The legislative branch is made up of Congress and government agencies. Article I of the Constitution founded the legislative branch and gives it the authority to make laws.

Executive Branch of Government
The executive branch ensures that laws are obeyed. The president of the United States is the head of the executive branch of government. The vice president, the president's cabinet, and heads of independent agencies assist the president.

Judicial Branch of Government
The judicial branch is made up of the court system. The highest court in the United States is the Supreme Court. Article III of the Constitution established the Supreme Court. Other federal courts were created by Congress.

Wars

Indian Wars	1500–1890s
French and Indian War	1754–1763
Revolutionary War	1775–1783
War of 1812	1812–1815
Mexican War	1846–1848
American Civil War	1861–1865
Spanish-American War	1898
World War I (The Great War)	1914–1918
World War II	1939–1945
Cold War	1945–1991
Korean War	1950–1953
Vietnam War	1957–1975
Persian Gulf War	1991
Iraq War	2003–2010

United States Marine Corps War Memorial

Economic Terms

bank	interdependence
barter	interest
bond	interest rate
business	international trade
checking account	invest
choices	investment
consumer	markets
credit	needs
debt	producer
demand	product
Department of the Treasury	recession
division of labor	regulations
economy	savings account
entrepreneur	scarcity
export	services
Federal Reserve bank	specialize
free enterprise	stock
goods	stock market
Great Depression	supply
human resources	taxes
import	trade
income	wants
inflation	

Canadian Provinces and Territories

Provinces

Alberta
British Columbia
Manitoba
New Brunswick
Newfoundland and Labrador
Nova Scotia
Ontario
Prince Edward Island
Quebec
Saskatchewan

Territories

Northwest Territories
Nunavut
Yukon

Mexico's States

Aguascalientes	Hidalgo	San Luis Potosí
Baja California	Jalisco	Sinaloa
Baja California Sur	México	Sonora
Campeche	Michoacán	Tabasco
Coahuila	Morelos	Tamaulipas
Colima	Nayarit	Tlaxcala
Chiapas	Nuevo Léon	Veracruz
Chihuahua	Oaxaca	Yucatán
Durango	Puebla	Zacatecas
Guanajuato	Querétaro	
Guerrero	Quintana Roo	

Inventors

Sibilla Masters
ca. 1670–1720
Designed a corn pulverizer that cleaned and cured corn; was among the first Americans to receive a patent

Benjamin Franklin
1706–90
Invented the lightning rod, the Franklin stove, and the flexible catheter; also created many social projects, including the first circulating library, a street-cleaning system, free elementary schools, a fire brigade, a police force, and a city hospital

Robert Fulton
1765–1815
Designed and built the first commercially successful steamboat

Eli Whitney
1765–1825
Invented the cotton gin; also invented a machine that could produce musket parts that were exactly alike, laying the foundation for mass production

Samuel F. B. Morse
1791–1872
Built the first American telegraph

John Deere
1804–86
Invented the first steel plow that efficiently turned American prairie soil

Cyrus McCormick
1809–84
Invented a mechanical reaper for harvesting grain, which greatly reduced the amount of farm labor needed in grain production

Levi Strauss
1829–1902
Along with Jacob Davis, invented riveted blue denim jeans and jackets

Elijah McCoy
1843–1929
Designed a lubricating cap that would automatically release oil onto train parts, making train travel more efficient

Alexander Graham Bell
1847–1922
Invented the first telephone; also invented a hydrofoil boat, an early iron lung, wax cylinders for recording machines, and a device that anticipated ultrasound

Ida Henrietta Hyde
1857–1945
Invented the microelectrode, a small device that stimulates a living cell and records the activity within that cell

James Naismith
1861–1939
Invented the game of basketball in 1891

Marie Curie
1867–1934
Discovered two radioactive elements, polonium and radium; Curie is the first person to win two Nobel prizes

Madame C.J. Walker
1867–1919
Created and sold a line of grooming products for African American women's hair

Wilbur Wright
1867–1912
Along with his brother, Orville, invented the power-driven airplane

Orville Wright
1871–1948
Along with his brother, Wilbur invented the power-driven airplane

Albert Einstein
1879–1955
Developed the theory of relativity, $E = mc^2$

Walt Disney
1901–66
Invented the multiplane camera in 1936.

Ruth Wakefield
1905–77
Invented chocolate chip cookies

Grace Murray Hopper
1906–92
Invented the first computer compiler in 1952

Bessie Blount Griffin
1914–2009
Invented an automatic invalid feeder; She received a patent for her invention in 1951.

Ruth Handler
1916–2002
Invented the Barbie doll

Bessie Nesmith
1922–1980
Invented Liquid Paper correction fluid

Robert Noyce
1927–90
One of two inventors of the integrated chip, or microchip

Joseph McVicker
1929–1992
Along with his uncle, Noah, McVicker patented Play-Doh modeling clay.

Space

Planets

Planet	Diameter (miles)	Distance From the Sun (miles)	Number of Moons
Mercury	3,032	36 million	0
Venus	7,521	67 million	0
Earth	7,926	93 million	1
Mars	4,222	142 million	2
Jupiter	88,846	484 million	16
Saturn	74,898	888 million	19
Uranus	31,763	1,784 million	17
Neptune	30,788	2,799 million	8

Space Terms

asteroid
astronomer
astronomy
axis
black hole
circumpolar stars
comet
constellation
eclipse
elliptical
galaxy
gas giants

gibbous
gravity
inner planets
meteor
meteorite
Milky Way
moon
North Star
orbit
outer planets
phases
planet

planetary system
probe
revolve
rotate
satellite
solar system
solstice
space
star
telescope
zenith

Animal Groups

Mammals

Animal	Group
apes	shrewdness
bats	colony
bears	sleuth, sloth
cats	clowder, pounce
cattle	drove, herd
deer	herd
elephants	herd
ferrets	business
giraffes	tower
gorillas	band
hippopotamuses	bloat
kangaroos	troop
lions	pride
monkeys	barrel, troop
oxen	team, yoke
porcupines	prickle
seals	herd, pod
squirrels	dray, scurry
tigers	streak
whales	gam, herd, pod
wolves	pack

Insects

Animal	Group
ants	colony
bees	grist, hive, swarm
caterpillars	army
cockroaches	intrusion
flies	business
gnats	cloud, horde
grasshoppers	cloud
hornets	nest

Birds

Animal	Group
birds	flight, flock, volary
buzzards	wake
chicks	brood, clutch
cranes	sedge
crows	horde, murder
doves	dule
eagles	convocation
finches	charm
flamingos	stand
gulls	colony
jays	party, scold
larks	exaltation
nightingales	watch
owls	parliament
parrots	company
partridge	covey
penguins	colony
quail	bevy, covey
ravens	unkindness
rooks	building
sparrows	host
storks	mustering
swallows	flight
teal	spring
turkeys	gang, rafter

Reptiles and Amphibians

Animal	Group
crocodiles	bask
frogs	army
snakes	nest
toads	knot
turtles	bale, nest

Fish

Animal	Group
bass	shoal
fish	draft, nest, school, shoal
herring	army
sharks	shiver
trout	hover

Animal Offspring

Animal	Young
alligator	hatchling
ant	antling
bear	cub
bee	larva
bird	chick, hatchling, nestling
buffalo	calf, yearling
camel	calf, colt
canary	chick
cat	kit, kitling, kitten
cattle	calf, stot, yearling
chicken	chick, cockerel, poult, pullet
cicada	nymph
coyote	pup, whelp
crocodile	hatchling
deer	fawn
dog	puppy, whelp
dolphin	calf, pup
dove	pigeon, squab
duck	duckling, flapper
eagle	eaglet, fledgling
elephant	calf
ferret	kit
fish	fingerling, fry, minnow, spawn
fly	grub, maggot
fox	cub, kit, pup
frog	froglet, polliwog, tadpole
giraffe	calf
goat	kid
goose	gosling
gorilla	infant
guinea pig	pup
hippopotamus	calf
horse	colt (m), filly (f), foal, yearling

Animal	Young
kangaroo	joey
lion	cub, lionet, whelp
monkey	infant, suckling, yearling
moose	calf
mouse	kitten, pup
muskrat	kit
opossum	joey
ostrich	chick
owl	howlet, owlet
partridge	cheeper
peacock	chick, pea-chick
pelican	chick, nestling
pig	farrow, piglet, shoat
platypus	puggle
quail	cheeper, chick, squealer
rabbit	bunny, kitten
raccoon	cub, kit
rat	kitten, pup
rhinoceros	calf
sea lion	pup
shark	pup
skunk	kitten
squirrel	kitten
swan	cygnet, flapper
tiger	cub, whelp
toad	tadpole
trout	fry
turkey	chick, poult
walrus	cub
whale	calf
wolf	cub, pup
woodchuck	cub, kit
zebra	colt (m), filly (f), foal

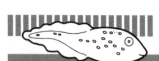

Animal Life Cycles

Frog

egg ➜ tadpole ➜ tadpole with legs ➜ froglet ➜ adult frog

Fly

egg ➜ larva ➜ pupa ➜ adult

Grasshopper

egg ➜ nymph ➜ adult

Butterfly

egg ➜ larva ➜ pupa ➜ adult

Fish

egg ➜ young fish ➜ adult

Chicken

egg ➜ hatchling ➜ chick ➜ chicken

Turtle

egg ➜ young turtle ➜ adult

Saltwater Crocodile

egg ➜ hatchling ➜ yearling ➜ juvenile ➜ sub-adult ➜ breeder

Plant Life Cycles

Plants

seed ➜ seedling ➜ young adult plant ➜ adult plant ➜ flower ➜ fruit

Trees

seed or pit ➜ seed ➜ seed with leaves ➜ seedling ➜ small tree ➜ growing tree ➜ mature tree with fruit that contains seeds

Food Chains

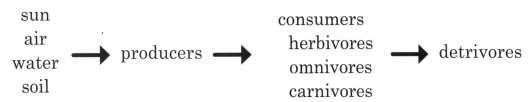

sun
air
water
soil
→ producers → consumers
herbivores
omnivores
carnivores
→ detrivores

Examples

sun ➝ grass ➝ antelope ➝ lion

flower ➝ caterpillar ➝ frog ➝ snake ➝ owl

tiny plants ➝ fish ➝ killer whale

tiny plants ➝ krill ➝ sea birds ➝ leopard seal

plants ➝ squirrel ➝ wolf

plants ➝ ants ➝ mouse

green plants ➝ insects ➝ fish ➝ big fish ➝ eagle ➝ bacteria

plants ➝ grasshopper ➝ toad ➝ snake ➝ hawk ➝ bacteria

algae ➝ small fish ➝ large fish ➝ sea lion ➝ shark ➝ bacteria

Plant and Animal Cells

Parts of a Plant Cell

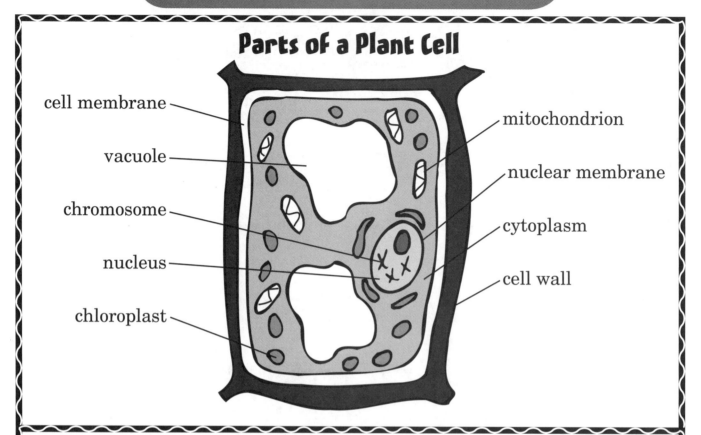

cell membrane

vacuole

chromosome

nucleus

chloroplast

mitochondrion

nuclear membrane

cytoplasm

cell wall

Parts of an Animal Cell

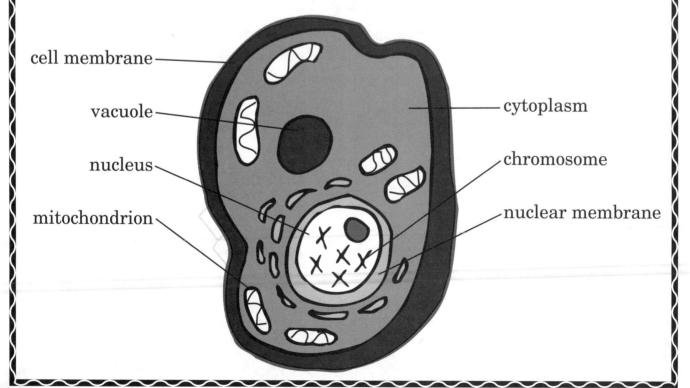

cell membrane

vacuole

nucleus

mitochondrion

cytoplasm

chromosome

nuclear membrane

Products Made From Plants

Plant Products

adhesives
chalk
cleansers
cosmetics
decorations
different types of
    cloth
dyes
food
fossil fuels
fragrances
furniture
inks
medicines
paint
paper
personal care items
rope
string
wax

Tree Products

cork
  bulletin boards
  coasters
  hot pads
  sound proofing
rubber
  boots
  elastic
  erasers
  machinery parts
  rubber bands
  seals
  surgical gloves
  tires
  toys
wood
  boats
  building materials
    floors
    house frames
    molding
  fuels
    charcoal
    firewood

furniture
  chairs
  desks
  lamps
  tables
musical instruments
  guitars
  pianos
  violins
paper
  decorations
  money
  toys
  wallpaper
  writing
sports equipment
  arrows
  bats
  golf clubs
  hurdles
tools
  handles
  ladders
  pencils
  rulers

Science

Habitats: Ocean and Freshwater

Ocean Animals

albatross
anemone
anglerfish
barnacle
blue whale
clam
cod
copepod
crab
dolphin
flying fish
gull
halibut
herring
krill
lobster
manta ray
marlin
mussel
octopus
porpoise
seal
shrimp
starfish
tuna

Ocean Plants

bayberry
beach pea
beach plum
cypress
palm
pine
plankton
sandspur
sea grape
sea grasses
seaside daisy
seaweed
wild rose

Freshwater Animals

beaver
beetle
crayfish
damselfly
dragonfly
duck
frog
goose
groundhog
heron
kingfisher
largemouth bass
mink
muskrat
newt
otter
platypus
snail
swan
toad
trout
turtle

Freshwater Plants

duckweed
figwort
flowering rush
meadowsweet
reed
water forget-me-not
water hawthorn
water hyacinth
water lily
yellow flag iris

The Ultimate Teacher's Book of Lists • ©The Mailbox® Books • TEC61339

Habitats: Forest and Desert

Forest Animals

bear
bison
bobcat
caribou
caterpillar
chipmunk
coyote
crow
deer
elk
groundhog
jay
ladybug
lemming
lynx
mountain lion
owl
raccoon
skunk
squirrel
timber wolf
vole
wolf
woodchuck
wood mouse

Forest Plants

buckeye
English bluebell
hickory
knapwood
magnolia
maple
oak
primrose
rosebay willowherb
vetch

Desert Animals

bobcat
centipede
coyote
fox
Gila monster
ground squirrel
hawk
hummingbird
jackrabbit
javelina
kangaroo rat
lizard
mule deer
owl
rattlesnake
scorpion
tarantula
tortoise
wasp
woodpecker
wren

Desert Plants

brittlebush
buckhorn cholla
desert marigold
fishhook barrel
 cactus
foothills palo verde
globe mallow
ocotillo
prickly pear
saguaro cactus
summer poppy

Habitats: Rain Forest and Grassland

Rain Forest Animals

ant
bat
beetle
bird of paradise
black panther
butterfly
chimpanzee
cockatoo
eagle
frog
howler monkey
jaguar
lemur
leopard
lizard
macaw
monkey
opossum
parrot
peacock
salamander
sloth
snail
snake
spider
termite
toucan
turtle

Rain Forest Plants

avocado
banana
bromeliad
cedar
coffee
cypress
lemon
lichen
moss
peanut
pepper
pineapple
pitcher plant
sawpalm
sesame

Grassland Animals

aardvark
antelope
Australian dingo
bison
black mamba
buzzard
cape buffalo
cheetah
coyote
elephant
gazelle
gemsbok
Geoffrey's cat
greater kudu
hyena
kangaroo
lion
Mexican kit fox
ostrich
pampas deer
prairie dog
rabbit
rattlesnake
rhinoceros
secretary bird
termite
wildebeest
zebra

Grassland Plants

climbing hempweed
elm
frog fruit
grass pink
love vine
oak
peppergrass
prickly pear cactus
red milkweed
thistle
tickseed
willow

Minerals and Rocks

mineral: a solid material that has particles arranged in a repeating pattern called a crystal

Examples: calcite, diamond, feldspar, mica, pyroxene, quartz, sulfur, talc, topaz

properties of minerals:

streak—the color of the powder left behind when you rub a mineral against a streak plate

luster—the way the surface of a mineral reflects light

hardness—a mineral's ability to resist being scratched

rock: material made up of one or more minerals

rock cycle: rocks constantly changing from one kind to another

igneous rocks

rocks that form when melted rock (magma) hardens

basalt
gabbro
granite
obsidian
peridotite
pumice

sedimentary rocks

rocks that form when layers of sediment squeeze together and get stuck over time

breccia
coal
conglomerate
flint
limestone
sandstone
shale
siltstone

metamorphic rocks

rocks that form when high heat and/or pressure causes changes in an igneous or a sedimentary rock

amphibolite
gneiss
marble
quartzite
schist
slate

Dinosaurs

Allosaurus

Anchisaurus

Ankylosaurus

Apatosaurus

Brachiosaurus

Brachyceratops

Coelophysis

Deinonychus

Diplodocus

Edmontosaurus

Iguanodon

Ischisaurus

Megalosaurus

Ornithomimus

Pachycephalosaurus

Parasaurolophus

Plateosaurus

Prosaurolophus

Protoceratops

Seismosaurus

Stegosaurus

Supersaurus

Triceratops

Troodon

Tyrannosaurus

Velociraptor

Matter

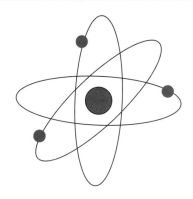

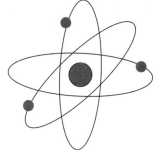

atom

mixture

chemical changes

physical changes

chemical reactions

physical property

combustibility

reactivity

condensation

solid

density

solubility

evaporation

solution

gas

state

liquid

volume

mass

weight

matter

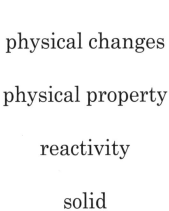

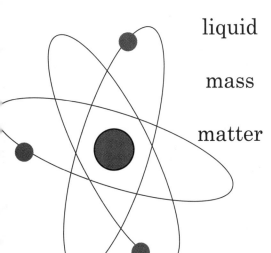

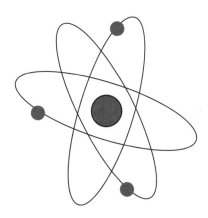

Simple Machines
tools used to make work easier

inclined plane: a flat surface that has one end higher than the other

lever: a simple machine with a bar that turns around a fixed point (fulcrum)

pulley: a simple machine made up of a wheel and a rope or belt

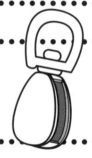

screw: made by wrapping an inclined plane around a pole

wedge: the edge of a smooth, slanted surface

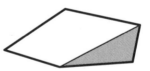

wheel and axle: a simple machine made up of a large wheel attached to a smaller wheel or rod

Electricity and Magnets

attract	magnetic force
battery	magnetic poles
charge	neutral
circuit	neutron
closed circuit	negative charge
conductor	open circuit
electric cell	parallel circuit
electric current	positive charge
electric field	proton
electromagnet	repel
electromagnetic	resistor
electron	series circuit
insulator	simple circuit
lightbulb	static electricity
magnet	switch
magnetic dipole	temporary magnet
magnetic field	wire

Weather

air
air pressure
almanac
anemometer
atmosphere
barometer
Beaufort wind scale
breeze
cirrus clouds
climate
cloudy
cold front
condensation
cumulonimbus clouds
cumulus clouds
dew
El Niño
evaporation
flash flood
flood
flurries
fog
freeze

frost
Fujita scale
hail
humidity
hydrometer
ice
isobar
La Niña
lightning
local winds
meteorologist
meteorology
mist
muggy
overcast
precipitation
prevailing winds

radar
rain
rainbow
rain gauge
ridge
showers
sleet
snow
sprinkles
storm
stratus clouds
sunny
temperature
thermometer
thunder
troposphere
trough
warm front
warning
water cycle
watch
wind
wind chill

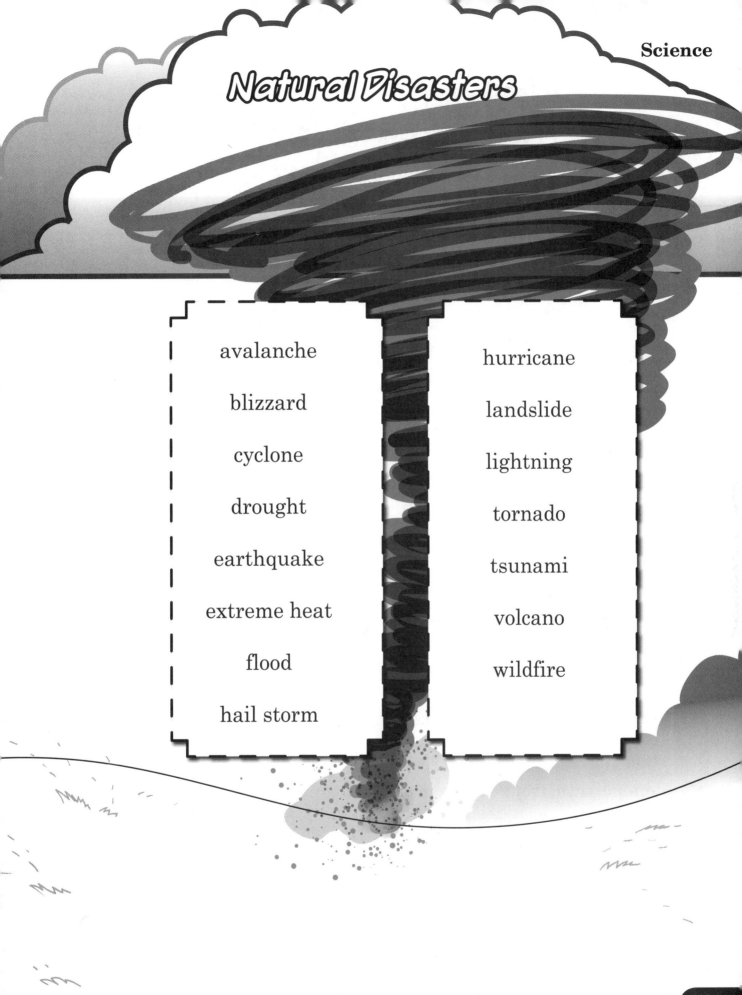

Natural Disasters

avalanche

blizzard

cyclone

drought

earthquake

extreme heat

flood

hail storm

hurricane

landslide

lightning

tornado

tsunami

volcano

wildfire

Science

The Human Body

cells: the building blocks of life

⬇

tissue: cells that work together to perform a certain function

⬇

organ: tissues that work together

⬇

system: organs that work together to perform a function

Body Systems

circulatory system: consists of the heart and blood vessels; moves blood throughout the body, taking food and oxygen to the cells and removing carbon dioxide and other wastes

digestive system: consists of the mouth, teeth, salivary glands, esophagus, stomach, small intestine, pancreas, gallbladder, liver, and large intestine; breaks food into substances the cells can use

muscular system: consists of more than 600 skeletal and smooth muscles; moves the body

nervous system: regulates and coordinates the activities of all the other body systems; made of three main parts

    central nervous system: consists of the brain and spinal cord; receives information from the senses, analyzes it, and responds

    peripheral nervous system: consists of nerves that carry information to the central nervous system (sensory neurons) and relay instructions from the central nervous system (motor neurons)

    autonomic nervous system: part of the peripheral nervous system; regulates automatic body functions

respiratory system: consists of the nose, trachea (windpipe), larynx (voice box), pharynx, and lungs; provides the body with oxygen and rids the body of carbon dioxide

skeletal system: consists of over 200 bones; supports the body, protects internal organs, and works with muscles to move the body

Nutrition: My Plate

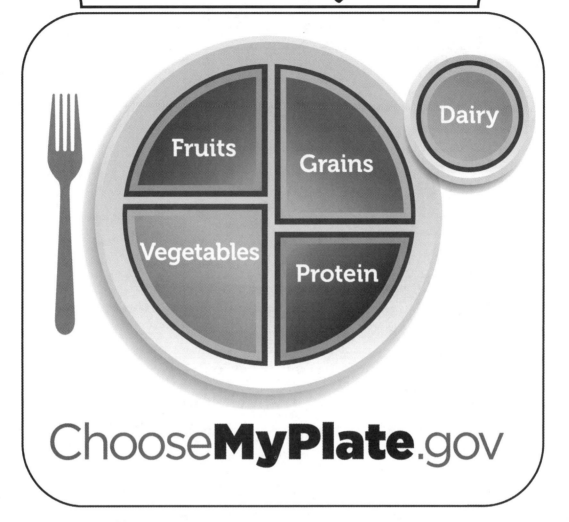

Food Group Examples

grains: breads, cereal flakes, crackers, grits, oatmeal, pasta, pitas, popcorn, rice, tortillas

vegetables: broccoli, carrots, lettuce, mushrooms, onions, peas, spinach, sweet potatoes, tomatoes

fruits: apples, bananas, berries, cherries, grapes, lemons, oranges, peaches, pineapple, watermelon

dairy: cheese, ice cream, milk, pudding, yogurt

protein: beef, chicken, dried beans, eggs, fish, nuts and seeds, pork, shellfish, turkey

Scientific Method

Ask a question.

Do background research.

Write a hypothesis.

Test the hypothesis with an experiment.

Analyze data and draw a conclusion.

Report results.

Science Tools

apron

balance scale

basin and bowl

beakers (glass and plastic)

calculator

clipboard

clock with second hand

compass

dropper

eyewash

fire extinguisher

first aid kit

flask

funnel

hand lens

hot plate

latex gloves

magnet

measuring cups

meter stick

microscope

microscope slides

mirror

petri dishes

safety gloves

safety goggles

spoons

spray bottle

telescope

test tube

thermometer

timer or stopwatch

video camera

weights

wire

Classroom Jobs

In the Classroom

alphabetizer: puts student papers in alphabetical order to assist teacher with record keeping

animal caretaker: tends to classroom pet(s)

attendance monitor: takes and records daily attendance

board cleaner: washes whiteboards, chalkboards, and/or overheads

caboose: last student in line; monitors the line from the rear

calendar helper: assists teacher with daily calendar activities

closet checker: checks closet or cubbies for tidiness; at the end of the day, checks to make sure all belongings have been claimed

desk monitor: periodically checks students' desks or table seats for tidiness

door holder: holds open and then shuts classroom doors and doors to other classrooms visited

flag holder: holds the flag and leads the class in the Pledge of Allegiance

greeter: welcomes new students and shows them around; introduces classroom visitors and explains any student work or classroom displays

homework monitor: assists teacher in collecting homework; helps classmates as needed

librarian: organizes classroom library

light monitor: turns on and off lights

line leader: first student in line

lunch count monitor: records the daily lunch count

media monitor: turns on and off classroom media and adjusts volumes as needed

messenger: takes notes and escorts students to the office or other classrooms as needed

paper collector: collects papers

paper passer: passes out papers

pencil sharpener: sharpens pencils

plant caretaker: tends to classroom plant(s)

recycling monitor: organizes classroom recyclable materials

restroom monitor: checks classroom or hallway restrooms to make sure that all students are out; one monitor for boys and one for girls

sink monitor: wipes up classroom sink and notifies teacher if soap and paper towels are needed

sweeper: sweeps and/or cleans items from the classroom floor

table captain: group leader for a table or group of desks

teacher's helper: assists teacher as needed

time keeper: sets classroom timer and gives teacher reminders about how much time is left for a task

weather monitor: checks and records the daily weather

Outside the Classroom

cafeteria monitor: wipes tables and sweeps the floor after lunch

hall monitor: monitors students' behavior in the hallway; reports to teacher

playground equipment monitor: responsible for taking out and collecting any playground equipment

special subject monitor: monitors classmates' behavior while in a special subject, such as art, music, and PE

Tasks for Parent Volunteers

Instructional Tasks

assist during writers' workshop

assist with art projects

assist with centers

help students with make-up work

help with computer activities

listen to students reading aloud

organize and prepare classroom manipulatives

play review games with students

read to the class

read with individual students

review flashcards, such as those for sight words and math facts

share personal materials or experiences that correspond with a lesson

Noninstructional Tasks

alphabetize class papers for teacher

assist with classroom book orders

attend assemblies

attend field trips

copy, laminate, or die-cut materials

email families with class news and reminders

fill students' take-home folders

find books to match a classroom theme

help in school library

organize classroom library

plan class parties

prepare art materials

prepare classroom games

put up bulletin boards

restock classroom materials, such as paper, crayons, and pencils

sharpen pencils

type class newsletter

update class website

Volunteer

Happy Elementary
"Where learning is fun!"

Miscellaneous

Words of Praise

Awesome!
Be proud.
Clever.
Dynamite work!
Excellent effort!
Fantastic!
Good for you!
Good going.
Good thinking!
Great job!
How wonderful.
I like this.

Just super!
Keep it up.
King-size work
Love it!
Marvelous!
Mighty effort
Neat!
Nice going.
Outstanding!
Perfect!
Quite good.
Right on.

Super!
Superb!
Terrific!
That's the way!
Tremendous work!
Unbelievable!
Very good.
Way to go!
Wow!
You did it.
You have the right stuff.
You're on the right track.

Incentives

Individual (not tangible)

choose the next class
    read-aloud book
extra computer time
first in line
lunch with the teacher
positive phone call home
read to class
sit next to a friend
sit next to the teacher
star student of the week
take home class mascot
teacher's helper

Class (not tangible)

dance time
earn table or group
    points
extra read-aloud time
extra recess
invite a mystery reader
    to the classroom
lunch with the teacher
movie
party
play a class game

Individual or Class (tangible)

award or ribbon
bookmarks
erasers
no-homework pass
pencils
stamp on hand
stickers
visit the prize box

Report Card Comments

Academic Achievement

____ has strengthened her skills in ____.

____ is maintaining grade-level achievements.

____ grasps new concepts and ideas readily.

____ takes great pride in all the work he does.

____ is having some difficulty with ____, but, if she continues to work hard, she will see improvement soon.

____ has great enthusiasm for everything we do in class. However, he is having some difficulty with ____.

____ reads quickly; however, she needs to focus more on comprehension.

There has been a noticeable improvement in ____'s study habits this reporting period!

Although ____ tries to do his best, he often has difficulty keeping up with the rest of the class.

I am concerned about ____'s progress. She has shown some improvement, but her growth does not reflect expectations for this point in the school year.

Citizenship

____ is a good classroom citizen. She is respectful and listens to others.

____ is a very helpful and dependable student.

____ is listening to directions more carefully.

____ is accepting responsibility well.

____ is friendly and cooperative with his classmates.

____ has a good attitude about school.

____ has a difficult time following directions and often needs redirection to complete a task.

____ is trying to practice good citizenship habits but needs to be more consistent.

____ needs to follow the classroom rules.

____ needs to improve his self-control so he can focus on classroom activities and tasks.

Work Habits

____ works well in both independent and group activities.

____ always uses her time wisely.

____ is enthusiastic about schoolwork and always puts forth his best effort.

____'s excellent attitude is reflected in the work she does.

____ does not use his time wisely in class. Because of this, the quality of his work is not as good as it can be.

____ needs to listen to all directions to complete tasks accurately.

____ needs to use his time constructively.

____ is doing grade-level work at this time. However, I am sure she can do even better! When she improves her ____, I know the work will improve.

____ must improve his work habits if he is to gain the fundamentals needed for ____ grade work.

When ____ is able to settle down, he does much better work. However, he often seeks the attention of his classmates, which causes distractions.

Field Trips and Emergencies

Keep these supplies on hand so you're prepared for field trips and weather-related emergencies.

✓ first-aid kit, including bandages, antiseptic wipes, disposable gloves, gauze, and medical tape

✓ hand sanitizer

✓ baby wipes

✓ resealable plastic bags

✓ cell phone

✓ up-to-date class list

✓ emergency contact list, including parent or guardian names and phone numbers and the school's phone number

✓ list of students who have allergies; copies of medical release forms; and needed medical supplies, such as an EpiPen auto-injector

✓ notepad and pencil

✓ digital camera

✓ flashlight

✓ bottled water

✓ packaged snacks, such as crackers or pretzels

✓ paper and crayons for students

✓ rain slickers

✓ sanitary napkins

✓ spare walking shoes

✓ weather radio

✓ At the beginning of the school year, ask each family to write a note to its child in the event of an emergency. The author of the note should encourage the child to be calm and assure him that you will keep him safe. Also encourage the writer to include a comforting family photo with the letter. Keep the letters in a safe place and distribute if needed.